D1001950

THE KEEN DELIGHT

HAROLD L. WEATHERBY

THE KEEN
DELIGHT

THE CHRISTIÁN POET IN
THE MODERN WORLD

ATHENS
THE UNIVERSITY OF GEORGIA PRESS

Library of Congress Catalog Card Number: 74–800–43
International Standard Book Number: 0–8203–0367–4

The University of Georgia Press, Athens 30602

Set in Linotype Garamond No. 3
Printed in the United States of America

FOR MY MOTHER

Contents

Introduction

In his essay on Dante, T. S. Eliot admonishes his readers to remember that there is a considerable difference between thirteenth-century Catholicism and modern Catholicism and that if we are to understand the *Divine Comedy* we must take that difference into account.[1] We might turn the matter the other way around and say that we must also take that difference into account if we are to understand the *Four Quartets.* Unfortunately Eliot does not say what he conceives that difference to be. Allen Tate, pursuing the same subject, is more helpful: "The Catholic faith has not changed since Dante's time," but "the Catholic sensibility," the mode of approach to that faith, has.[2] In what respect, we may ask, does the sensibility differ? How does Newman's theology differ from Aquinas's; how does Hopkins's and Eliot's poetry differ from Dante's?

I have not selected these names at random. Newman and Aquinas are both wellsprings from which theological poets in their respective ages have drunk; and their waters have radically different tastes. Aquinas recast Christian theology at a crucial moment in the Church's history and by doing so gave Christians a new mode of approach to the doctrines in which they had always believed. That fact has long been acknowledged by intellectual historians.[3] However, we are just now beginning to recognize that Newman, at another crucial moment, did much the same thing. Notice, for instance, Christopher Dawson's comment that when the religious history of the nineteenth century is finally written, "there is no doubt that the personality and genius of Newman will be seen as a key point of the whole development." Dawson's interpretation of that development and its origin seems valid: that at the end of the eighteenth century the "Catholic Church was a venerable structure which seemed tottering and decadent. Then came the Revolution, and at its impact the whole edifice of traditional ecclesiasticism crashed in ruin and destruction." Yet at the death of Leo XIII a century later, "the Church was stronger than it had been since the seventeenth century." "It was the mission of Newman," Dawson adds, "to be the philosopher and interpreter of this Christian renaissance."[4]

Let us say then that we are dealing with two moments of reconstruction in the history of Christian thought, upon each of which a theologian of major proportions has left his distinct mark. Dante wrote in the ambience of the Thomist renaissance; Hopkins and Eliot, though with differing degrees of immediacy, in the sphere of Newman's influence. It is to the distinction in sensibility between those two moments of renaissance that we may ascribe the differences between medieval and modern Catholicism to which Eliot and Tate allude. Dawson's brief remarks indicate his awareness that the Church after the Revolution was different in many respects from the "venerable structure" which lasted from the middle ages to the end of the eighteenth century. He calls Newman (by which, of course, he signifies his theology) "at once the embodiment and the contradiction of the spirit of his age."[5] That statement rewards careful scrutiny, for it helps us to define the Newmanist sensibility in opposition to the Thomist. To be the embodiment of the spirit of the nineteenth century is to be at home in the world of Coleridge, Carlyle, Tennyson, Arnold, and Pater. It means, among other things, to be a philosophical sceptic, to appeal to heart and conscience rather than to intellect for knowledge of God and for the grounds of theology. To be the contradiction of that spirit is to be the thorny dogmatist who demolished that wholly unambiguous embodiment of the age—Charles Kingsley. Newman was both at once, with the consequence that he is on one hand as antique as Augustine, on the other as modern as James Joyce. It is that curious combination of effects—of dogmatic belief and philosophical scepticism in particular—which he insinuated into the

Catholic revival of the nineteenth century and which he communicated thereby to Hopkins and Eliot.

That is as far as generalities will take us. Now we must ascertain precisely how it is that Newman's theology differs from Aquinas's, Hopkins's and Eliot's poetry from Dante's. The key to that difference is to be found in their respective theories of knowledge and belief, and as prelude to a careful examination of those theories it will be helpful to state Aquinas's position.

The Angelic Doctor teaches that there are three ways to know God or, as Maritain puts it, three wisdoms.[6] The first wisdom is metaphysical, the effect of reason. The second is theological, the third mystical; and both of these are the effects of faith. Metaphysical wisdom is drawn from, quite literally abstracted from, man's sense impressions of the external, physical creation. It presupposes the Pauline doctrine that the invisible things of God are known from the things which are made, that God is present in His immensity as cause of all created things and can be discerned by the unaided reason in all things. St. Thomas's five proofs might be regarded as demonstrations of how such metaphysical wisdom is acquired. Both theological and mystical wisdom differ from metaphysical wisdom in that they are revealed by faith (and one must remember that faith is a supernatural virtue) rather than acquired by reason. There is nevertheless a profoundly important distinction between these two latter wisdoms, for even though theological wisdom issues from the same source as mystical wisdom, its mode of expression is identical with metaphysics. That is because, as Aquinas says, "the thing known is in the knower according to the mode of the knower,"[7] and the mode of knowledge for man in this life is abstraction. In short both metaphysics and theology are conceptual or notional whereas mysticism is, in Maritain's word, practical. Both the wisdom acquired by reason and that given by faith are in one respect knowledges or sciences—acquisitions of the intellect and therefore, by definition, conceptual. Mystical wisdom, on the other hand, is not something known, but something experienced, *"according to a mode that is suprahuman and supernatural,"* which differs from both metaphysics and theology in being "no longer a question of merely learning, but rather of suffering divine things."[8]

How one either learns divine things by faith or suffers them in charity we shall see in due course. It suffices for the moment to suggest that whereas Aquinas's and Dante's work is informed by a profound understanding of all three wisdoms (though both the *Summa* and the *Comedy* are metaphysical and theological in emphasis) Newman (who is the embodiment as well as the contradiction of his anti-intellectual age) largely distrusts the metaphysical because it is abstract and notional. Consequently he tends to confuse theology with mysticism. It is as though theology were suspended in a state of delicate balance between metaphysics and mysticism, drawn to mysticism by a common source in faith and to metaphysics by a common subjection in the conceptual reason. Therefore it is not surprising that when, under the antimetaphysical influences of his age, Newman rejected the natural reason as an adequate means of demonstrating God's existence, his theology should be drawn away from knowledge toward experience. Both on account of Newman's influence and on account of their common exposure to the same apostate age, Hopkins and Eliot in their poetry move in the same direction as Newman in his theology. However, in the case of Eliot, as we shall see, the gravitation toward experience at the expense of knowledge is redeemed by a discovery of what true mystical wisdom is.

In light of these considerations we may say that one aspect of that difference between medieval and modern Catholicism to which Eliot and Tate allude—and perhaps the most important aspect for poetry—is the difference in modes of knowing God. Moreover because the medieval, the Thomist, mode incorporates a broader range of human experience than the modern, because it embraces both reason and faith, both knowledge and experience, whereas the modern tends to place its whole emphasis on faith interpreted as experience, we can best understand the latter by seeing it as a fragment of the former. William Butler Yeats's parody of "Dover Beach" comes to mind:

> Though the great song return no more
> There's keen delight in what we have:
> The rattle of pebbles on the shore
> Under the receding wave.
>
> ("The Nineteenth Century and After")

The poet's delight is always in what he has, in what is sufficiently real for him that he can make poetry from it. The *Comedy* is as good an example of the great song to which Yeats alludes as one can imagine, and it is clear that Dante, because of his debt to St. Thomas, *had* a great deal more than Newman, Hopkins, and Eliot. The modern shift of emphasis from reason to experience imposes a sharp limitation on the scale of Catholic theology and poetry. Whereas Dante has at his disposal a comprehensive and intellectually consistent image of the cosmos and of its relationship to God, Newman, Hopkins, and Eliot tend either to leave the creation out of account, to treat it as an obstacle to the knowledge of God, or to regard it as a medium of God's felt presence rather than of knowledge. Consequently whereas Dante is able to deal with God intellectually—as He is demonstrated by reason and understood by theology—Newman, Hopkins, and Eliot (though in varying degrees) are inclined to substitute intimations of immortality for a true science of the holy.

Let us begin then by showing what Dante had, in what he took a keen delight. By doing so we shall put ourselves in a position to see what Eliot means when he distinguishes Dante's Catholicism from his own. We can then understand better than we have thus far both the *Comedy* and the *Quartets*.

The Scale of the Comedy

WHEN critics discuss the intellectual and religious resources that Dante could draw upon, the emphasis is usually on the medieval image or "model" of the universe which he held in common with most of his contemporaries.[1] What is often neglected in such discussions is the fact that that image of the cosmos is informed, in the literal, Scholastic sense of that term, by metaphysical and theological wisdom and that the poem culminates in a transition from the knowledge to the experience of God. The true significance of Dante's cosmology is not the image of the creation which it provides but rather the metaphysical and theological knowledge of God which it gives and the mystical experience of Him to which it points. That does not mean that Dante is a Platonist—that he thinks the function of the physical creation is merely to represent spiritual things symbolically (or, in Newman's term, economically). On the contrary he had learned from Aquinas that the visible world is a reality in its own right. However, he had also learned from the same source that it is an intelligible reality which reveals its nature and its cause to the human intellect in terms of concepts which, raised by faith to a far higher level of understanding, become the matter of Christian theology.

It is instructive to see how Dante is able to begin with a physical object and without any diminution of its natural reality see God, metaphysically and theologically, in and through it. Consider, for instance, his consistent use of the sun from the beginning to the end of the *Comedy*. The emotional content of the first few lines of the "Inferno" is carefully calculated to convince us of the sun's importance to Dante as a source of physical light and warmth; anyone who has been lost in the woods at night knows what is happening in these opening lines. We see first the *selva oscura* (the dark wood), and it does not take more than a casual reading for us to realize that this is a place of literal darkness and visceral terror. We see at the same time that the right way which has been lost is a spiritual as well as merely physical way, so we know that the darkness and terror are also spiritual. *Tant' è amara che poco è più morte* (so bitter is it that death is hardly more);[2] to say such a thing about a merely physical wood would be to voice an emotion in excess of fact. The phrase serves to make the necessary transition between the physical and spiritual levels of Dante's experience, and it does so with such perfect economy and such profound effect that in less than ten lines he has put himself in a position to convince us that the virtues of the sun are likewise both physical and spiritual. Indeed, if they were not, the sun's appearance could not serve, as in fact it does, to dispel the whole terror. When he allows us to see its rays clothing the shoulders of the hill at the dark valley's head, we feel with him relief from both physical and spiritual darkness. Because Dante has been able to convince us that the *selva oscura* is a dark and terrible condition of the soul, we are prepared to transfer our immediate emotional reaction to the sun's appearance to the level of its spiritual significance. Moreover, lest there be any question about that transference, Dante supports the emotional effect of the contrast with a powerful rhetorical antithesis. In line three we are told that the dark wood is the place where the *diritta via era smarrita* (where the straight way was lost) and, in line eighteen, that the sun is the planet which *mena dritto altrui per ogni calle* (leads men straight on every road).

Having thereby established the sun's dual significance, Dante proceeds to develop that significance in terms of the poem's cosmological symbolism, and he does so in such a fashion as to provide a controlling pattern of contrasts for the entire *Comedy*. On account of the emotional effects of the opening lines the reader is prepared thereafter to look upward and to look toward light, toward the sun in particular, for help and salvation—in a word, for God. If we interpret that upward looking metaphysically we may speak of the reader's being directed by the emotional impact of Dante's imagery to discern God's presence in His created effects. If we wish to speak theologically, in terms of revelation, we may transfer the same emotions and the same direction of thought to God's presence by grace, as light, in the darkness of the human soul; he is, after all, the orient, the "dayspring," the "light to them that sit in darkness." Whether we speak metaphysically or theologically we speak of God as known in concept, not of God as experienced in charity; and the effect of Dante's imagery is not to diminish the conceptual accuracy of theological and metaphysical wisdom but rather to accommodate our emotional reactions, drawn from physical experience, to our knowledge. It is that accommodation which the controlling pattern of metaphoric contrasts effects in the course of the poem.

In the "Inferno," for instance, the *cieco mondo* (blind world) where "all light was mute" (v, 28), Dante refers us repeatedly, in one way or another, to the "sun and other stars." The damned refer repeatedly to the "bright life," *la vita serena,* the life lived under the sun; and the periodic references to the time of day, by which we are allowed to plot the journey, are invariably in terms of movements of the heavens with their various lights. These references to the great light-bearing wheels of the cosmos are carefully calculated to punctuate the darkness of hell, itself an extension and deepening of the *selva oscura,* with much the same emotional intensity and therefore, by implication, with the same metaphysical and theological meaning, which the sun offers Dante in the first canto. Many of these allusions require no more than a word or two, but their effect is to recall us to the central contrast between light and darkness, at once visible and spiritual (metaphysical and theological) on which the poem is built. Cavalcanti's question about his son is a case in point. He does not merely ask whether Guido is still alive; he couches the question in an allusion to the sun in both its physical and spiritual significance, and in doing so he asks, probably without realizing it, both about his son's physical and spiritual life: *non fiere li occhi suoi il dolce lome?* (x, 69: Strikes not the sweet light on his eyes?) We cannot read the question without recalling how the "dolce lome" of the sun, which leads men aright, strikes Dante's eyes in the dark wood; and in this particular instance the association is made doubly intense by what we know of Dante's friendship with Guido and by the fact that in Florence they had walked very nearly the same via.

Cavalcanti's question is only one of many similar instances. Dante's conversation with Brunetto Latini is another. Here, too, the contrast between hell and the "bright life" is drawn in such a fashion that we are prepared to give it full emotional assent, and in this instance Dante's conversation specifically recalls the previous sharp contrast between the wood and the sun. Brunetto walks in his baked flesh beneath a rain of fire, "mourning [his] eternal loss" (*Inf.*, xv, 42). Against the backdrop of such a picture and such a phrase, Dante speaks of *la vita serena* (the bright life) and tells Brunetto how *mi smarri' in una valle, / avanti che l'età mia fosse piena* (I lost my way in a valley before my age was at the full), and, by contrast, how, at morning, *le volsi le spalle* (I turned my back upon it) (49–52). Brunetto, in his prophecy, picks up the same thread of metaphor and develops it further, in such a fashion as to sharpen the contrast between the damned and the saved, between those for whom the sun in its threefold significance— physical, metaphysical, and theological—is eternally mute and those, like Dante, who are being led toward it out of the *cieco mondo:*

> Ed elli a me: 'Se tu segui tua stella,
>   non puoi fallire a glorïoso porto,
>   se ben m'accorsi nella vita bella;
> e s'io non fossi sì per tempo morto,
>   veggendo il cielo a te così benigno,
>   dato t'avrei all'opera conforto.'   (55–60)

(And he said to me: "If thou follow thy star thou canst not fail of a glorious haven, if I discerned rightly in the fair life, and had I not died too soon, seeing heaven so gracious to thee I would have strengthened thee in thy work.")

To speak of following one's star to a safe haven is to run the risk of triteness; however, if we have followed the pattern of Dante's sun and darkness imagery thus far and understood its spiritual implications, the risk is no more than that. By this point in the poem we are in no doubt what Dante's star is or what his port will be. We know that the planet which leads men the right way and which, with the other stars, offers a visible manifestation of the invisible things of God in the things which are made, is leading Dante to the *glorïoso porto* of the empyrean heaven, to the beatific vision. Moreover, that vision is nothing less than an immediate experience (like mystical wisdom but exceeding it in glory) of the very God who is known through the dark glass of concepts drawn metaphysically from our sensible impressions of the sun and other creatures or revealed theologically by faith, which appropriates the same natural concepts for its utterance. The irony involved in Brunetto's statement is that he refers to Dante's star, his journey, and his success in merely mundane terms. We might even venture the guess that the irony established by the diverse points of view serves as one measure (in addition to his sin of sodomy) of Brunetto's damnation; certainly it suggests an absence of metaphysical and theological understanding as well as a considerable measure of pride in his own accomplishments as Dante's teacher. The irony in no way diminishes the effect of the central symbolic contrast between the sun and the darkness. In fact the limitation of Brunetto's understanding, the fact that he and Dante speak on different levels, serves to point by contrast the spiritual significance of *la vita serena*.

There are numerous similar instances in the "Inferno" in which Dante invokes the sun or stars, not only as sources of natural light but also as symbols of God. They are both at once and not less the one for being also the other, because according to St. Thomas's philosophy the sun and stars along with all created things literally manifest God. The only other instance of this symbolic pattern which we need to cite is that which appears in Ulysses's account of his journey, and this particular passage is important because it prepares us for Dante's transition from the *cieco mondo* to the bright world. In the course of his narrative Ulysses punctuates hell's darkness with an allusion to *tutte le stelle . . . dell'altro polo* (xxvi, 127: all the stars of the other pole). For Ulysses, on account of his sin, these lights are tokens of destruction and of the loss of heaven. However, his allusion prepares us for Dante's subsequent view of those same stars at the foot of the purgatorial mount, and for Dante, of course, they have the same significance that the sun has throughout the *Comedy*. These stars of the *altro polo* are the first lights which he sees when he passes Satan at earth's center and begins his long ascent to heaven; and they are harbingers of the full light with which the "Paradiso" ends. More immediately these *cose belle / che portà'l ciel* (xxxiv, 137–38: beautiful things that Heaven bears), when Dante first glimpses them, come to him, and to us, with the same sweetness as the sun to the *selva oscura.* After the horrors of Judecca, *a riveder le stelle* (139: to see again the stars) carries the emotional conviction necessary to support the metaphysical and theological significance of these lights. That significance is insisted upon at the beginning of the "Purgatory," as soon as Dante reemerges into the world of the sun; for now he sees the *quattro stelle / non viste mai fuor ch'alla prima gente* (i, 23–24: four stars never seen before but by the first people)—stars associated with man's primal blessedness and appropriate as a prelude to the recapturing of that blessedness.

They are prelude, also, to the sun, with whose rising Dante begins his ascent of the mountain; nor can we escape the similarity between the beginning of the "Inferno" and the beginning of the "Purgatory." In both instances the sun, the sensible manifestation of God in the order of the cosmos, leads Dante out of dark places into light. As more than one critic has suggested, the mountain at the head of the dark valley at the beginning of the "Inferno" anticipates the mount of Purgatory. Dante can only make the ascent, can only follow the sun, by taking what Virgil calls the long way. He must descend first into those regions, at once physical and spiritual, where the sun is mute. Indeed we might say that at the beginning of the "Purgatory" the *Comedy* commences again. There is one sense in which Dante is now exactly where he was thirty-five cantos earlier, but on account of his descent into hell he is in a different relationship both to the cosmos and to God who made it and who declares Himself in it than he was before. Again we see the great symbolic importance of Ulysses's story; for Ulysses has attempted to come to the sunny mountain the wrong way, the short way, and in doing so he violates the order of metaphysical and theological wisdoms. Thus he loses the sun, loses God, forever. Because Dante has been humble and obedient he is now able to walk in the sun's power; and the divine significance of that power is perfectly sustained through the whole course of the purgatorial ascent, a journey which is controlled by the movements of the sun.

II

Thus far we have considered the sun and stars of the *Comedy* as symbols of God only in a very general sense. Indeed we have given little more than lip service to the words *metaphysical* and *theological,* which we must now investigate in detail. Let us begin with the latter, for in the *Comedy* the former can only be properly understood in terms of it.

It is perhaps Dante's greatest accomplishment that he is able to represent the full ramifications of Catholic theology in his cosmological symbols. The sun is more than simply a manifestation of the invisible things of God in a thing which is made. It is, more precisely, a presentation in symbolic form of God the Son, the Wisdom or the Word eternally begotten of the Father. Consider again the references to the sun in canto I of the "Inferno":

Temp'era dal principio del mattino,
  e'l sol montava 'n su con quelle stelle
  ch'eran con lui quando l'amor divino
mosse di prima quelle cose belle.   (37–40)
(The time was the beginning of the morning and the
sun was mounting with those stars which were with it
when Divine Love first set in motion those fair things.)

In other words the sun is in the ram, with those stars which
were with him when God first set the whole creation in mo-
tion. *Quelle cose belle* anticipates the *cose belle / che porta'l
ciel* at the very end of the "Inferno," and in both instances
the fair things are associated with the act of creation and with
man's primal innocence. Moreover, it is in terms of that asso-
ciation that the theological implications of the images begin
to ramify. According to Christian theology God the Son, the
Wisdom, the Word of God, made the world. He is the perfect
image of the Father, and He made the whole cosmos accord-
ing to that image so that all things in it reflect Him. More-
over, in the fullness of time, to save man from his sins, that
same Son, Word, Wisdom, took flesh in the womb of the
Blessed Virgin Mary; and the Annunciation by which the In-
carnation was accomplished took place on March 25 when the
sun again was in the ram with all the *cose belle* in their pri-
mal places. Finally that same Son, Word, Wisdom, suffered
death upon the cross for man's salvation, to restore man to
the beauty which the sun and other stars, moved by His love,
have never lost but which man by his sin has marred. Since
Good Friday also occurs when the sun is in the ram and the
stars in their pristine order, Dante by his seasonal allusion
unites the Creation, Incarnation, and Crucifixion—all three be-
ing appropriately represented by the sun which the Son has
made and by which, in its light and movements, He declares
the glory of the Father, whose image He is, in whose image he
made all things and to whose image He restores man by His
Incarnation and death.

From these considerations we see immediately that Dante is preparing us at the very beginning of the poem for its ending. When in the last canto of the "Paradiso" he discerns the likeness of man "painted" upon the reflected light of the second circle and recognizes that his own desire and will are moved by *l'amor che move il sole e l'altre stelle* (xxxiii, 145: the Love that moves the sun and the other stars), he has shown us, in effect, the restoration of man by Christ's passion to the perfect harmony of spiritual motion which is represented sensibly by cosmological motion and to the sublimity of supernatural light which is manifested sensibly in the light of the *cose belle*. In other words, as we now begin to see, the cosmological symbolism is so deftly controlled that with it Dante is able to represent visibly the theological concepts of the Word or logos, of the Creation, of the Incarnation, of the Passion, and of the fruits of the Passion—the Resurrection and Ascension, both of our Lord and through Him of all men in the rectification of their wills and desires. Moreover, as we also now recognize, we are never allowed to see the sun or stars or to hear mention of "the bright world" without catching at least a momentary glimpse of the vast theological backdrop of the poem. The sweetness of light penetrating the dark wood or overwhelming Dante at the foot of the mountain is nothing less than the sensible manifestation, by virtue of nearly perfect metaphor, of the sweetness of Christ.

Perhaps the best instance in the *Comedy* of the use of cosmological symbols to express theological wisdom is to be found in the tenth canto of the "Paradiso." It is the canto in which Dante enters the sun's sphere, and it is there, appropriately, that the sun's theological significance is fully demonstrated. Our first indication that Dante has ascended from the sphere of Venus is an allusion, not to the sun, but to the Son and, through Him, to the Father and to the Holy Ghost:

> *Guardando nel suo Figlio con l'Amore*
> *che l'uno e l'altro etternalmente spira,*
> *lo primo ed ineffabile Valore,*

> quanto per mente e per loco si gira
> con tant'ordine fè, ch'esser non puote
> sanza gustar di lui chi ciò rimira.   (1–6)

(Looking on His Son with the Love which the One
and the Other eternally breathe forth, the primal and
ineffable Power made with such order all that revolves
in mind or space that he who contemplates it cannot
but taste of Him.)

We recognize, as soon as we read these lines, that Dante is
invoking a complex of difficult concepts—God's paternity, His
filiation, His spiration, and the relationship between His trini-
tarian nature and the creation. This, in short, is the language
of pure theology, and Dante's task as a poet is to translate
these concepts into images without diminishing their notional
force. Somehow he must make us *see* in symbols what, in fact,
can only be understood or known.

He takes as his point of departure for doing that a facet of
the very doctrine he is demonstrating—that God the Holy
Trinity has so made the world that He can be "tasted" in all
that revolves, whether in mind or space. Dante is here pur-
suing to its logical conclusion the meaning of the cosmos which
he has been insisting upon from the very beginning of the
poem. We have seen already that the sun is to be understood
as the light of Christ both as creator and redeemer. Here, in
the sun's own sphere, Dante extends that understanding to in-
clude the relationship between the Son and the Father and the
Spirit. That we may perceive that ineffable mystery in the *cose
belle,* Dante tells us to lift our eyes to that part of the uni-
verse, of the *alte ruote* (lofty wheels), *dove l'un moto e l'altro
si percuote* (where the one motion strikes the other) (*Par.,*
x, 7–10). The "one motion" is the ecliptic; the other is the
celestial equator. The point of their conjunction is the very
point at which Dante first found the sun (the Son) in the
selva oscura. Now that he is literally *in* the sun rather than
surveying it from a distance, it is appropriate that he should
perceive the mystery of the Trinity which has been implicit

from the first in that planet which leads men the right way. He conveys that perception indirectly, through the eyes of St. Thomas Aquinas, who is aptly described as one of "the fourth family of the Father on high," whose joy is God's *mostrando come spira e come figlia* (*Par.*, x, 51: showing how He breathes forth and how begets). The emphasis here is on the "showing," the *mostrando*—the understanding rather than the suffering of divine things. It is by understanding or knowing that Aquinas and the other holy doctors in his circle *taste* the Holy Trinity in all that revolves, and it is appropriate that they express their joy in that knowledge by dancing in a circle around Beatrice and Dante. They revolve, Dante tells us, like ladies in a dance and *come stelle vicine a' fermi poli* (*Par.*, x, 78: like stars near the steadfast poles). The latter image recalls the whole circling pattern of the universe, and it suggests specifically the two great motions whose intersection has become for Dante, in reference to the sun, a signature of God. The movement of the sun and other stars is the movement of delight in Him whose paternity, filiation, and spiration is the satisfaction of all creatures. The giration of the theologians is the movement of delight in the *knowledge* of that paternity, filiation, spiration, and satisfaction.

III

One aspect of that knowledge is specifically metaphysical, and it is appropriate that it should be; for metaphysical wisdom both anticipates and supplements theological wisdom. It anticipates theology, for God is present in His immensity, as cause, before He is present by grace as redeemer; consequently we must know Him in some degree metaphysically before we can proceed to the understanding which theology gives us. It supplements theology, for, as we have seen, it provides the concepts by which we understand those things revealed by faith. For instance, when we speak of God as Three Persons in one Substance, we employ a concept, *substance,* drawn from metaphysics, to explain the revelation of God's trinitarian nature.

Similarly, when we speak as Dante does of the relationship between the creation and the redemption of the world, we are in effect supplementing revealed wisdom concerning creation, redemption, and grace with knowledge of God as cause which is drawn from metaphysics. In other words we gain a proper theological understanding of redemption from a proper metaphysical understanding of God's relationship as cause to the world He redeemed. Therefore if we are to comprehend fully what Dante means when he says that God can be tasted in all that revolves in mind or space, we must see how metaphysics unites with theology in Dante's imagery.

Before we can understand that union, we must see first exactly what metaphysics is; for it attaches itself to theology simply by being what it is. It is the "science of being as being," and whereas theology describes the nature of God and His relationship to His creatures in such personal terms as love and justice, metaphysics describes that same relationship in terms of the nature of being. Fundamental to St. Thomas's (and Dante's) metaphysics is the proposition that God is pure existence, being itself, *ipsum esse,* and that from Him all created being, partial being, depends. Another way to state the same proposition is that God may be defined as simply "to be," whereas all other beings whatsoever are limited by some complement of that infinitive. "To be man," "to be angel," "to be tree," "to be dog," is less than simply "to be"; and the limitation which defines the species of being implies by contrast that pure, unlimited *esse* which is the origin of all those varieties of creatures which are defined by their limitation. The latter are contingent beings, and within that category fall all the species which constitute the cosmos—the angels, the heavens, men, beasts, plants, stones. All these are in a state of potentiality, and it is their defining limitation, the complement of "to be," which keeps them from pure actuality. To be man is necessarily to be in potentiality in respect to the fullness of being, for the extent of being itself is obviously greater than that comprised by any species. Only God is in a state of pure actuality because He not only embraces the fullness of being in Himself: He *is* that very fullness. He is *actus purissimus sine ulla potentialitate;* therefore any being which is only a partial act of being and which therefore possesses, is defined by, a measure of potentiality is necessarily dependent on God, on pure act, for its existence. We can say that God is present to every creature as its cause; that is what we mean by His immensity. Or we can say that in God all creatures exist in their origins, for in His being is their root or source. Thus we recall that, as an aspect of his vision of the Holy Trinity at the end of the "Paradiso," Dante sees in God, *legato con amore in un volume, / ciò che per l'universo si squaderna* (bound by love in one volume, that which is scattered in leaves through the universe). There he sees the *sustanze e accidenti e lor costume* (substances and accidents and their relations) which constitute the whole creation, *quasi conflati insieme, per tal modo / che ciò ch'i' dico è un semplice lume* (as it were fused together in such a way that what I tell of is a simple light) (*Par.,* xxxiii, 86–90). In effect he here sees from within, at the very source of their existence, the various members of the cosmos, the *cose belle,* which he has seen from without during the long upward journey. Moreover his seeing them in this fashion, as it were under a divine aspect, makes it clear to us how and why, when he had seen them from without, God was manifest in them; because their very being derives from God and, if their being, naturally their "taste."

From these considerations we may proceed to an examination of the way in which metaphysical and theological wisdoms are united in Dante's imagery. Theology teaches us that all creatures are drawn to God as their source and end; Thomist metaphysics teaches us that each species of creature is drawn to being itself in its own proper way and that that way is determined by its nature or act of being.

To understand how that is so we must recognize that God created not parts but a whole composed of parts and that He is the source and end of each of those parts by virtue of being the source and end of the whole. "Now if we wish to assign an end to any whole, and to the parts of that whole, we shall find, first, that each and every part exists for the sake of its proper act, as the eye for the act of seeing." Hence we may conclude that in the cosmos "every creature exists for its own proper act and perfection" (*ST,* 1, 65, 2). As we have seen, the act of every creature defines that creature's species or identity in the whole chain of contingent being; God alone is pure act, pure existence, *ipsum esse.* It follows that the more complete the act of a creature's being and the less limited by potentiality, the closer he approaches to the perfect "to be" *sine ulla potentialitate* which is God. Furthermore the closer he approaches to that perfection the higher his place in the hierarchy of the cosmos, in which Seraphs stand at the top. Thus we see that when a man, Dante in this instance, takes his proper place in the harmonic unity of the cosmos, he is, in effect, becoming fully and completely what he is—man.

However, God has so made man that he can only become fully and completely what he is by grace; and it is here that theology and metaphysics meet. Intellectual creatures, men and angels, are so constituted that they literally cannot be what they are except when they participate in a union with God which is effected by His grace. Therefore for man, who has fallen from grace, to "exist for [his] own proper act and perfection" in the whole of created being, he must be restored or redeemed. Only then, when his being is moved in harmony with the beings of the sun and other stars, can he participate in the perfection of the whole.

The relationship between theology and metaphysics can also be understood in terms of their respective explanations of how God is the creature's source and end. Theology teaches that God is love; metaphysics teaches that God is *ipsum esse.* Both theology and metaphysics teach that God is simple, not composite, and that in Him all attributes or qualities are one simple undifferentiated existence: that perfect being and perfect love are one in Him—that He is, without differentiation, both. It is on account of that wonderful simplicity that the great chain of being is also the fair chain of love, and that just as the higher creatures in that chain possess, by definition, a fuller measure of being and a smaller measure of potentiality, they likewise are capable of possessing and enjoying the love of God in fuller measure than the lower creatures can. That is why, in being redeemed by grace to fulfill his own proper act or perfection of being, man is likewise made capable of enjoying that considerable measure of God's love for which he was created. It is therefore altogether appropriate that when Dante, restored by grace to the enjoyment of that love, sees the acts of being of all creatures united in God's pure existence as in their source, he also sees them as united in love; for that source, that pure existence, is love, and he, because he now participates in it, can perceive all things in its light:

> *Nel suo profondo vidi che s'interna,*
> *legato con amore in un volume,*
> *ciò che per l'universo si squaderna.*
>
> (*Par.*, xxxiii, 85–87)

It is also appropriate that he believes that he has seen the being of the cosmos as a whole, *la forma universal di questo nodo* (the universal form of this complex), because, in telling of it, "I feel my joy expand" (*Par.*, xxxiii, 91–93). That joy is explained by what follows—the vision of God as the three circles of light and of the union of God and man in the second circle. The joy Dante feels is his love given in response to that love which moves all that revolves both in mind and space —that love which the Father and the Son, beholding one another, eternally breathe forth; that pure love which is also pure being and, therefore, the uncaused cause of all love and of all being; that love which is seen and tasted both in the act of being of each creature and in the ordered whole of the cosmos, in which, bound by love, those acts, those loves, subsist. To be redeemed by grace is to be united to that perfect love which is also perfect being, and the only possible way to comprehend the fullness of that experience is in the sweet consent of metaphysics and theology. It is Dante's remarkable achievement that he has been able to convey that consent in image.

Dante never allows us to forget the concurrence of being and love or of the respective wisdoms which perceive them. Consider his analogy between the rising of fire and the rising of the soul or intellect to God. It is inherent in its act of being for fire to rise; by rising it takes its proper place in the order of the whole of being. It is likewise inherent in man's act of being to ascend "in thought and mind" to God; in that ascent, by grace, he too, as we have seen, takes his proper place. In the first canto of the "Paradiso," in which Dante ascends from the earthly paradise to the sphere of the moon, Beatrice is constrained to explain to him how such an ascent is possible:

> *Tu non se' in terra, sì come tu credi;*
> *ma folgore, fuggendo il proprio sito,*
> *non corse come tu ch'ad esso riedi.*   (*Par.,* i, 91–93)

(Thou art not on earth as thou thinkest, but lightning flying from its own place never ran so fast as thou returnest to thine.)

Lightning, of course, is fire; and fire's *proprio sito* is above earth, water, and air. Likewise the *proprio sito* of man, both in respect of his proper act of being and of his redemption by grace, is "above"—in union with God. Therefore Beatrice compares the two, illustrating that which moves in mind by allusion to that which moves in space and, in doing so, employing metaphysics and theology in conjunction. Indeed, without St. Thomas's metaphysical system, without the firm assurance that the cosmos is an order of being contingent in every particular upon God as perfect being, the metaphor would fail and the theology of Dante's redemption would cease to be intelligible in terms of the whole of being. However, Dante holds that system so firmly in his grasp that he is free to vary the analogy for effect, by inverting its terms. Dante, says Beatrice, is rising to his proper place just as rapidly as lightning is flying from its own. For fire to fall it must be under some constraint which violates its being and its place in the cosmos. Dante has already violated his own being by sin and, in the *selva oscura,* has departed from his proper place. Now through grace he returns to it. The inverted comparison makes it possible for Dante to recapitulate the whole significance of the journey in three lines.

Lest Dante, or we his readers, be left in any doubt about the true meaning of this analogy between the being of fire and the soul of man, Beatrice proceeds to explain the matter in detail. To begin with, she reiterates the recurrent motif, both of St. Thomas's theology and of his metaphysics, that it is the order among the creatures who constitute the hierarchy of being *che l'universo a Dio fa simigliante* (that makes the universe resemble God). In that order, she adds, *sono accline / tutte nature, per diverse sorti, / più al principio loro e men vicine* (all natures have their bent according to their different lots, nearer to their source and farther from it). Then she makes the same point in an interesting metaphor:

> *onde si muovono a diversi porti*
> *per lo gran mar dell'essere, e ciascuna*
> *con istinto a lei dato che la porti.*   (*Par.,* i, 105–114)
> (they move, therefore, to different ports over the great
> sea of being, each with an instinct given it to bear it
> on.)

These various "instincts" which are given to each creature to bear it to its particular port in the "great sea of being" are the properties which we have been discussing—of fire to rise, of water to fall. Beatrice goes on to illustrate her point with another reference to the property of fire: *Questi ne porta il foco inver la luna* (this [its "instinct"] bears fire up towards the moon). She adds that it is the interaction of these "instincts" or what she now calls these *permotore* or movers which holds the world together—*la terra in sè stringe e aduna* (binds the earth together and makes it one). She proceeds to the analogy between the instincts or properties of subrational creatures and the corresponding *permotore* inherent in the angelic and human acts of being: *nè pur le creature che son fore / d'intelli-genza quest'arco saetta, / ma quelle c'hanno intelletto ed amore* (*Par.*, i, 115–20: and not only the creatures that are without intelligence does this bow shoot, but those also that have intellect and love). The bow which shoots is, of course, the creature's particular act of being which determines its proper port in the great sea, its place in the great chain. It shoots each creature, each in its way, toward God who as Creator of all species and source of all being is also the end for which all creatures exist and the object of all loves.

Toward that end, that most perfect act of being itself, that love which moves all things, that object both of metaphysical and theological wisdom, that "joyous mark," that *sito decreto* (*Par.*, i, 124: place appointed), Dante, says Beatrice, by the bow of his being, strung as it were by grace, is now being shot. He is no more to wonder at his rising than at the fact that water, "freed from hindrance," as he is now freed from sin, falls (*Par.*, i, 139–40). It is an indication of the consistency and completeness with which Dante has transmuted this fusion of metaphysical and theological concepts into poetic symbol that once analogies like that of rising fire or falling water are established, he is able to allude to them later in the poem in such a fashion as to recall the whole pattern of doctrine on which they rest. For instance, in canto 10 of the "Paradiso" Aquinas uses the same metaphor to illustrate his own perfect freedom in God's will. He says to Dante that if he should refuse wine from the vessel of his wisdom to satisfy Dante's thirst, he "would be no more at liberty than water that does not fall to the sea" (88–90). He is saying in effect that his will and desire are moved by the perfect love (the fruit of grace in the soul) which moves all things, each in its proper order within the whole of being. In fact his allusion to the sea as the ultimate destination (or *proprio sito*) of water recalls, in the analogy, Beatrice's earlier allusion to the great sea of being in which each individual creature, by virtue of its nature, has its port. That sea may be a metaphor for the whole of created being, whose intrinsic end, says St. Thomas, is its own metaphysical order; or it may signify God, its extrinsic end, who is existence itself. It is the latter interpretation which is most probable, and it is certainly the latter which strengthens Aquinas's metaphor in canto 10. For if the literal sea is the *proprio sito* of water, the metaphorical sea of being (and of love) is man's proper home. The original metaphor ramifies and, in doing so, extends the implications of the intellectual system on which it rests.

One other such extension is worth noting and serves well to conclude these illustrations of the link in Dante's imagery between metaphysics and theology. I refer to one of Dante's most famous lines and one which, though usually quoted out of context, is if properly understood seminal to the whole interlocking pattern of the two conceptual wisdoms. It is the famous summary line in Piccarda's discourse on God's will and man's peace in which she explains to Dante that it is *formale ad esto beato esse* (essential to this blessed state) to keep oneself within the divine will (*Par.*, iii, 79). Sinclair translates *formale ad* as "the very quality of"; Grandgent, whom I have followed here, suggests "inherent in" or "essential to."[3] Neither translation quite hits the mark (though Grandgent is closer) because neither catches the concept of *form* which is implicit in Piccarda's metaphor. *Form,* of course, is really a name for a thing's act of being; the name of the form is the complement of the infinitive "to be." "To be water" is to have the form, water, as source or principle of being. Once that fact is understood we see that Piccarda's use of *formale* links her statement to the whole pattern of metaphor which Dante has been developing. Perhaps no single English word will suffice; for what any just translation must convey is that the formal quality of our blessed state is also its essence, that fully to be what one is and to occupy one's proper place in the chain of existence is to be blessed. Once we have grasped that point, we see that the *formale* recalls the various forms of fire and water which are fresh in the reader's mind when he meets Piccarda. Moreover, to keep those earlier allusions fresh, Dante allows Piccarda to expand upon them in her explanation. After showing him that "our rank from height to height through this kingdom is pleasing to the whole kingdom, as to the King who wills us to His will," *e'n la sua volontade è nostra pace* (and in His will is our peace), she adds that *ell'è quel mare al qual tutto si move* (it is that sea to which all things move) (*Par.,* iii, 85–86). That is the sea of being on which all things seek their respective ports, or to which water falls, depending on the metaphor before us. Suffice it to say that the metaphors are complementary, for they rest on the same metaphysical assumptions. The symbolic language of the poetry becomes what, for lack of a better word, we might call the dramatization of the intellectual system which undergirds it.

IV

From these considerations it should be clear that Dante possessed and took keen delight in, held as reality, a vision of existence sufficiently comprehensive to embrace not only all that moves in mind and space, but also God who creates and moves all. It is also clear that he embraced this vision in such a way that his theology is perfectly interpreted by his metaphysics and his metaphysics completed and brought to fruition by his theology. For that fusion of the two he was indebted, as all acknowledge, to St. Thomas—as he is also for the presence in the *Comedy* of mystical wisdom, of which we shall have more to say in chapter 5. That wisdom crowns the "Paradiso," and it is appropriate that it should; for just as the beatific vision, there signified, is the fruit of man's earthly and purgatorial pilgrimage, so mystical wisdom, even in this life, is the fruition of knowledge and belief. It is also appropriate that at the moment when the experience of the ineffable begins, poetry —especially a poetry like Dante's whose chief function is to express concepts—should cease. However, there is a very close link between the poetry of conceptual knowledge and those last few lines in which poetry seeks to convey divine experience; and that too is appropriate because mystical wisdom is best understood as subsisting at the paradoxical moment in which metaphysics and theology are left behind and yet are residual in our thought. Indeed the rich interlocking tracery of theology and metaphysics which is the burden of Dante's imagery carries the eye constantly upward to this point of ultimate concentration in which the pattern is completed by being swallowed up in something inestimably grander than itself. From the first moment that we see the sun in the dark forest and sense, though ever so vaguely, that its significance is spiritual, we are being drawn to this moment in which Dante no longer merely sees and knows but *is* the light. Without this moment Dante's grasp of the reality of God would not be full, his delight not keen, his poetry not complete. But without the metaphysics and the theology, this moment would not be.

Newman and Aquinas:
Metaphysics

WHEN we turn from a reading of the *Summa* and the *Comedy* to the *Apologia*, the *Idea of a University* or the *Grammar of Assent*, we are struck at once by a constriction of range —by a diminution in "what we have" and hence in the capacity for "keen delight" in God. The cause of that constriction and diminution (we have suggested it already) is Newman's distrust of metaphysics—his scepticism concerning the ability of the unaided reason to abstract a valid conceptual knowledge of God from sense experience of the physical creation. A careful examination of Aquinas on this matter will help to define Newman's limitations by contrast.

That the human intellect derives knowledge or science from sensible things St. Thomas proves by rejecting two extreme positions, with both of which, as we shall see in due course, Newman has certain affinities. One is the "materialism" of Democritus who believed that *"all knowledge is caused by images issuing from the bodies we think of and entering into our souls"* (*ST*, 1, 84, 6; italics in original: St. Thomas is quoting Augustine). The other is the "idealism" of Plato, who held that since the intellect is "an immaterial power" and "distinct from the senses" and "since the incorporeal cannot be affected by the corporeal," the intellect cannot possibly derive knowledge from sensible things but must rely instead upon a direct "participation" of separate intelligible forms, which it holds as "innate species." The only function of the sense impression, according to Plato, is to "rouse the intellect to the act of understanding"; however, what the intellect understands when thus aroused is not something derived from the senses but something resident from before birth in itself (*ST*, I, 84, 6).

In preference to these two extreme opinions St. Thomas chooses Aristotle's mean, and in that choice he defines his epistemological position. Aristotle and Aquinas agree with Plato, against Democritus, that the intellect and the senses are different from one another, "that the intellect has an operation which is independent of the body's co-operation," and that "nothing corporeal can make an impression on the incorporeal" (*ST*, I, 84, 6). However, they disagree with Plato in their insistence that the soul does not possess innate species but must derive the forms by which it knows from the composite substances that constitute the visible world which the senses apprehend. The doctrine of innate species is "unreasonable" on several counts: "first, because, if the soul has a natural knowledge of all things, it seems impossible for the soul so far to forget the existence of such knowledge as not to know itself to be possessed thereof"; second, "if we suppose that it is natural to the soul to be united to the body, . . . it is unreasonable that the natural operation of a thing [the soul's intellection] be totally hindered [as Plato's theory of innate species implies it is] by that which belongs to it naturally"; finally, our everyday experience proves "that if a sense be wanting, the knowledge of what is apprehended through that sense is wanting also: for instance, a man who is born blind can have no knowledge of colours" (*ST*, I, 84, 3). Therefore, St. Thomas, with Aristotle, concludes that the soul at birth is a blank tablet and that the *principium nostrae cognitionis est a sensu* (the principle of our knowledge is in the senses) (*ST*, I, 84, 6).

However, given Aristotle's "middle course" another problem arises; for since "nothing corporeal can make an impression on the incorporeal," how is it possible that the apprehensions of the senses can cause knowledge in the intellect? The answer, in effect, is that they do not: the intellect is the power that causes knowledge; and that is as it should be, for that which is more fully in act operates upon that which is more nearly in a state of potentiality. Therefore "according to Aristotle, the impression caused by the sensible does not suffice, but something more noble is required, for *the agent is more noble than the patient*" (*ST,* I, 84, 6; italics in original: St. Thomas is quoting Aristotle). However, that which is "more noble," more fully in act, is not an innate species but rather a capacity of the intellect whose property is to abstract intelligible species from sense impressions. This capacity is what is known in Scholastic terminology as the "agent intellect" or "active intellect," whose activity draws the potentially intelligible forms of all things into act and, in the process, makes the things themselves actually intelligible. However, since those potentially intelligible forms are not, as Plato taught, separate spiritual substances or Ideas but rather the forms of composite substances, it follows that they can only be apprehended by abstraction from those substances. Moreover, since it is the senses which apprehend the composite substances, it follows that knowledge is indeed derived from sensible things. Therefore St. Thomas concludes that "on the part of the phantasms, intellectual knowledge is caused by the senses," but that "since the phantasms cannot of themselves affect the passive intellect," we must recognize the necessity of the active intellect so that through its operation the potentially intelligible forms of all things may be made actually intelligible (*ST,* I, 84, 6).

From these epistemological doctrines we may isolate two points which are closely related to one another. The first is that the composite substances which constitute the physical creation are potentially intelligible or, as Etienne Gilson says, that St. Thomas does not consider the material world wholly material.[1] The second is that given this potential intelligibility of material things it is possible for the intellect literally to unite itself with, become one being with, the thing which it knows. Let us consider each of these assumptions in turn.

In the first place we must ask how it is possible for the material world to be intelligible—how it is possible for composite substances to be knowable. The answer lies in St. Thomas's doctrine of forms to which we have alluded already:

that the form of a thing is a thing's act of being, its to be. One consequence of that teaching is Aquinas's insistence, in opposition to what he calls the Platonist error, that the forms of created things have a real as well as an ideal existence. He does not deny their ideal existence, for he teaches that the forms of all things exist as ideas in the mind of God, as exemplars— just as the idea of a house exists in the mind of the architect before it is transmitted to brick or wood, or as the idea of a statue exists in the mind of the sculptor before it is made physically visible in stone. In God these forms subsist in the perfect simplicity of His pure existence, and their presence there is explained in the metaphysical doctrine that the source of all created being is in God. However, these forms also have real existence in the composite creatures who, taken together, constitute the physical creation. That is so because, even as exemplars in the mind of God, the form must be the form *of* something as, in man, the form of the body is the soul.

St. Thomas's discussion of the relationship between soul and body is a good index to his whole conception of form and to how he differs in this matter from the Platonists. The point which, from a Platonist's perspective, seems most shocking and the point upon which the Thomist conception turns is that "inasmuch as the soul is the form of the body, *it has not an existence apart from the existence of the body,* but by its own existence is united to the body immediately" (*ST*, I, 76, 7; italics added). The proposition needs to be repeated and its implications absorbed fully: the soul, the form of man, "has not an existence apart from the existence of the body"; and, we might add, that is true of its existence in the mind of God, at the very source of being, for God did not create souls and bodies as separate substances but as a single substance, just as the architect always imagines the house as brick or wood. (It is interesting in this regard that when Dante sees the exemplars of all creation in God, he sees, not pure or separate forms, but "substances and accidents" in their relationship to one another.) The soul "has not an existence apart from the existence of the body"; the form of anything has not an existence apart from the existence of that thing of which it is the form. (We need not enter fully here on the matter of the separation of soul and body in death; that is, after all, a question of theology rather than of metaphysics. Suffice it to say that St. Thomas regards that separation as contrary to nature and as remedied by the supply of the spiritual body.)

The Platonist error is to think of the form as having a separate existence which is altogether independent of the physical or composite being of which it is the form. Thus in the case of man the Platonist thinks of the soul and the body as having separate existences and of the soul's being united to the body "merely as its motor" (*ST,* I, 76, 8). This opinion, as St. Thomas shows, leads to all kinds of philosophical errors. For instance, if the body and the soul have separate existences, it is necessary to account in some fashion for the existence of the body; and if we hold such a view we are constrained to posit another substantial form, beside the soul, to account for the body, or we are forced to believe that "primary matter was some actual being—for instance, fire or air, or something of that sort," an opinion which is manifestly absurd, for it leads to an infinite regression (*ST,* I, 76, 4). Moreover, the Platonist position ultimately undermines all true science, including the science of metaphysics, for by separating the intelligible form from the thing of which it is the form (as the soul from the body) it makes knowledge of the thing impossible. The Thomist universe is material and intelligible at once, precisely because no such separation occurs.

It is that intelligibility, the fruit of the inseparability of form and thing, which makes possible the second fundamental assumption in St. Thomas's epistemology—that it is possible for the intellect literally to unite itself to the thing which it knows. That union is made possible by the intelligible species, as the following passages make clear.

Consider St. Thomas's statement that "the soul knows external things [*res quae sunt extra animam*] by means of its intelligible species" (*ST,* I, 85, 2). At first glance this proposition might seem to deny the real union between knower and thing known for which Aquinas is in fact arguing. He seems to be distinguishing between the *species* and the *things* with the implication that the former are subjective, in the soul, while the latter are *extra animam*. If that were in fact the case, the soul would not seem to be able to know the thing but merely a subjective reflection of the thing. However, it is precisely that separation of knowledge and thing known which St. Thomas seeks to avoid, and our key to a proper understanding of his meaning is the word *species*. The species is not what is understood, but that *by which* the thing outside the soul is understood: "it must be said that the intelligible species is related to the intellect [*se habet ad intellectum*] as that by which [*ut quo*] it understands" (*ST,* I, 85, 2). In other words the species is not to be regarded as the image or subjective representation of the thing, in distinction from the thing itself, but rather as the particular aspect of the thing which is intelligible, which is "related to the intellect as *that by which* it understands." Therefore the species which the agent or active intellect abstracts from the phantasm, because it is at once intelligible and "of the thing," affords the intellect a genuine knowledge of the thing.

To put the same matter another way we can say that the species is the presentation to the intellect, or the "intention" in the intellect, of the form of the thing known; that it is by means of the intelligible species that the form of a thing known is united to the form of the knower. It is at this point in the discussion that we come to see how integrally connected St. Thomas's various teachings are, that his doctrine of the structure of being directly informs his doctrine of the nature of knowledge. Were the form a separate substance, as Plato believed it to be, and were it possible as a consequence for the intellect to participate it directly by means of an innate rather than an acquired species, then it would be possible to separate the species from the *res,* and knowledge of the former would not guarantee knowledge of the latter. However, since the form has no separate existence but is the act of being of a composite substance, it follows that by its union with the form (as species) the intellect *must* enter into a union with the *res* of which it is the form and thus achieve a true science of the thing *extra animam*.

The same proposition can be stated in a variety of ways, and the very variety helps us to grasp the ramifications of St. Thomas's position. We can say, for instance, that the species which gives knowledge is inseparable, except by abstraction in the process of intellection, from the thing of which it gives knowledge. Therefore if we must call the species a mental image of the thing, which in some sense it is, we must insist that it is a mental image which unites the mind directly to the thing of which it is the image. Another way to express the same relationship is to say that the species is what the intellect understands secondarily whereas *id quod intelligitur primo est res cujus species intelligibilis est similitudo* (*ST*, 1, 85, 2: that which is understood first is the thing of which the intelligible species is the likeness). Etienne Gilson seems to be saying exactly the same thing when he defines the species as the immaterial and intelligible element in the *res* which makes the *res* "assimilable to a thought." The word *assimilable* catches St. Thomas's meaning exactly, for, as we have seen, knowledge means that the knower enters into a real union with the form of the thing known. Thus, in Gilson's words, "to know a thing is to become it."[2] Indeed we must not allow the imagination to intrude upon our efforts to understand this process of cognition, for if we begin to think imaginatively, we shall inevitably begin to think of a spatial separation between the intellect and the species. To do so is to distract ourselves, for the "operation which we are analyzing takes place entirely outside of space."[3] The union of the *res* and the *anima* by means of the species is an intellectual rather than a physical union, and if we allow spatial conceptions to creep into our thought on this matter we are forced into a distinction between reality and knowledge in which the process of abstraction gives us only a subjective substitute for the thing rather than the thing itself. Let us remember that the species is not an image in the usual sense, not an equivalent or substitute for the thing it reflects, but rather, in Gilson's words, "the very object [thing] under the mode of species."[4]

Thus we may say unequivocally that knowledge by means of the species, as St. Thomas understands it, is real knowledge, true science. However, there is one further term to be examined and one further relationship to be explained before the process of cognition can be fully understood. I refer to Aquinas's use of the word *concept* (sometimes *notion* or *intention*) and to the relationship between the species which the intellect abstracts from the phantasm of the *res* and the concept of *res* which, by virtue of the species, the intellect in turn produces. The matter is crucial for our present purposes, for Newman's distrust of metaphysical wisdom is a direct consequence of his distrust of the validity of concepts or notions.

St. Thomas explains the relationship between concept and species in the following manner: "We must further consider that the intellect, having been informed by the species of the thing, by an act of understanding forms within itself a certain intention of the thing understood, that is to say, its notion [concept], which the definition signifies." He proceeds to define this notion or concept as "a terminus of intelligible operation" and, for that reason, as "distinct from the intelligible species that actualizes the intellect . . . though both are a likeness of the thing understood."[5] The question which immediately presents itself is whether the notion or concept is a legitimate "likeness of the thing understood," for if it is not, we shall be forced into the very division between reality and knowledge from which St. Thomas's definition of the species rescues us. Gilson states the whole matter very clearly: in the process of intellection we deal with a twofold likeness of the thing known; the first likeness, the species, is the resemblance of the thing's form and a "direct likeness" because it is "not a representation of it but its promotion and, as it were, its prolongation"; the second likeness is that "which we conceive in ourselves and which is not the form itself but nothing more than its representation." It was that representation which Newman distrusted. Was his distrust warranted, or is there some way "to guarantee the fidelity of the concept to its object"?[6]

St. Thomas answers the latter question affirmatively and thereby delivers the concept from the status of a mere subjective reflection which may not adequately represent the thing (*extra animam*) which it reflects. The basis for his answer is the relationship between the intellect and the species which we have already examined: in the process of intellection the species is united to, becomes one with, the knowing subject. On account of that union it is possible for the intellect to form a concept, intention, or notion of the thing which represents, infallibly, the thing itself; whereas if the species were not a means of uniting the *res* to the *anima* but itself merely a reflection in the intellect, the intellect could not form an accurate concept of the thing. "For, by the fact that the intelligible species, which is the form of the intellect and the principle of understanding, is the likeness of the external thing, it follows that the intellect forms an intention like that thing, since such as a thing is, such are its works" (*CG,* I, 53). The last clause of that statement is crucial, for it signifies that the intellect, being brought into act by the form of the thing, is, in a sense, that thing—is "such as" that thing. Therefore by expressing its own being it expresses that thing. The concept it forms in that act of expression is infallible.

As St. Thomas says in another place, "since everything is true according as it has the form proper to its nature, the intellect, in so far as it is knowing, must be true, so far as it has the likeness [species] of the thing known, this being its form, as knowing." Thus we can say that "truth is defined by the conformity of intellect and thing" (*ST,* I, 16, 2), and the concept which expresses that conformity expresses the truth of the thing. The thing's form (as species) becomes the form of the intellect "as knowing"; therefore the concept, by expressing the intellect "as knowing," necessarily expresses the thing. As Gilson states the relationship, "the concept is not the thing; but the intellect, which conceives the concept, is truly the thing of which it forms itself a concept." Indeed the metaphor implicit in the word *conceives* brings us to the very heart of the matter; for the species is like seed which impregnates the mind, the notion or concept being the issue of that impregnation and utterance thereof. "It is this," says Gilson, "which confers objectivity upon our conceptual knowledge. The full weight of this doctrine, therefore, rests upon the two-fold aptitude of our intellect, first, to become the thing, and secondly, to bring forth the concept while thus being fecundated."[7]

Therefore because the concept or notion is a direct expression of the thing itself, it is possible to rely upon the intellect's intentions as legitimate representations of reality. Dante, as we have seen, does rely on them and thus becomes the poet par excellence of metaphysical wisdom. His images—of rising fire and falling water, of the sun and other stars—represent in visible form the intellect's concepts, and one virtue of his imagery is that it represents those concepts without diminishing their accuracy as concepts. Moreover Dante's range of metaphor extends to concepts of invisible as well as of visible things, and indeed the very definition of metaphysical wisdom is a discernment of the invisible things of God in the things that are made. How then, we may ask, is it possible for the unaided human intellect, from the species of creatures, to form concepts, not only of the creatures, but also of God who made them?

That it *is* possible Aquinas leaves no doubt: though "some truths about God exceed all the ability of the human reason" and must therefore be given to man by revelation as theological wisdom—such as "the truth that God is triune"—there are other truths about God "which the natural reason also is able to reach" (*CG*, I, 3). Among the latter are such truths as the fact of His existence and the fact that "as the first cause of all things" He exceeds all things which He causes. Moreover once we apprehend the fact that He is the first cause of all things, we can perceive that "creatures differ from Him, inasmuch as He is not in any way part of what is caused by Him; and that creatures are not removed from Him by reason of any defect on His part, but because He superexceeds them all" (*ST*, I, 12, 12). It is clear that these are the very sorts of knowledge about God which inform the imagery of the *Comedy* and which, throughout the poem, supplement and enrich Dante's strictly theological understanding. The very mention of these kinds of knowledge which fall into the category of metaphysical or natural is the first step toward understanding how such knowledge, such "facts" as God's existence and His causality, are acquired. For if we consider them carefully, we shall see that each of these "facts" is, as it were, a name for an effect of God's being; and St. Thomas bases metaphysical wisdom on the premise that "God is known by natural knowledge through the images of His effects" (*ST*, I, 12, 12).

That proposition, apparently so simple, entails the whole of Thomist metaphysics and epistemology; all we have said thus far inheres in it. In the first place, the human intellect can derive a natural knowledge of God from "the images of His effects," only because He is in fact present in those effects. That presence and its mode we know; it consists in the doctrine of form. Because the forms or principles of being of all created things are mixed with potentiality, they are held in existence, contingent upon the pure act of being, the *actus purissimus sine ulla potentialitate,* which is God Himself. Thus, as their cause, as pure existence, God is present in all created things: "Now since God is very being by His own essence, created being must be His proper effect; as to ignite is the proper effect of fire. Now God causes this effect in things not only when they first begin to be, but as long as they are preserved in being. . . . Therefore as long as a thing has being, God must be present to it, according to its mode of being" (*ST*, I, 8, I). Moreover that presence of God in created things is almost inexpressibly profound and intimate: it is at the very root of their existence. As St. Thomas puts it, since "being is innermost in each thing and most fundamentally inherent in all things since it is formal in respect of everything found in a thing, . . . hence it must be that God is in all things, and innermostly" (*ST*, I, 8, I).

It is that innermost presence that makes it possible for God to be understood from an understanding of His effects, and the link between the two understandings is the doctrine of the intelligible species which we have just examined. Let us recall that that species, which is the *quo est* in the act of intellection, is properly understood as the promotion of the form of the thing in the knowing intellect, by which the intellect is impregnated, brought into act. Therefore since God, as *ipsum esse* and as cause of all created *esse,* is present, *innermostly,* to the form, it follows that when the knowing intellect, through the species, becomes that form, by doing so it also unites itself to God whose existence and presence sustain the being of that form. Hence the concept or notion which expresses the union of the knower and thing known may also, by extension, express the thing known in relationship to God as its cause. It is in that way that St. Thomas interprets St. Paul's dictum about invisible things being manifest in things made, and we now see that his interpretation transcends the Augustinian or Platonic reading of that famous scripture; for St. Thomas's epistemology offers us, in the way we have described, a true science of God derived from his metaphysical effects. On account of those teachings Gilson can describe the Thomistic world as "a sacred universe," as an "enchanted universe," as "a world of beings, each one of which gives testimony of God by the very fact that it is": a world "impregnated to its every fibre with the intimate presence of a God whose supreme actuality preserves it in its own actual existence."[8] That, we recognize, is also the world of the *Comedy.* It is clearly not the world of Catholic theology and poetry in the nineteenth and twentieth centuries.

II

The vast difference between those two worlds owes a great deal to the fact that Newman and his fellow modern Catholics disagree with Aquinas that the concept or notion can be literally "of the thing."

Consider, for instance, the following statement from the

Grammar of Assent: "Now apprehension . . . has two sub-ject matters: according as language expresses things external to us, or our own thoughts, so is apprehension real or no-tional."[9] It is clear at a glance that such a distinction, from a Thomist point of view, must be regarded as a false dilemma. St. Thomas, could he have read Newman's statement, would probably have asked, "Why may not the notion (concept or intention), though admittedly 'our own thought,' be also an expression of 'things external to us,' of the *res extra animam?*" As we have seen from our examination of St. Thomas's episte-mology, it is the fidelity of notion to thing on which the possi-bility of genuine knowledge rests. To separate the one from the other and to ascribe different modes of apprehension to each is to drive a wedge between knowledge and thing known, between subjective and objective reality, which destroys science altogether.

That is the wedge that Newman drives, and not in this passage only but repeatedly in the *Grammar of Assent* and elsewhere. He speaks, for instance, of "individual propositions about the concrete" being "diluted or starved into abstract no-tions" (*Grammar,* p. 25). He refers to "two modes of thought," both of which have as their basis "the informations of sense and sensation," but which differ radically "in their results." "In the one we take hold of objects from within them [real apprehension], and in the other we view them outside of them; we perpetuate them as images in the one case, we transform them into notions in the other" (*Grammar,* p. 27). The dis-tinction between *transform* and *perpetuate* serves very well to indicate how radically Newman disagrees with Aquinas: for if a notion *transforms* the *res extra animam,* it clearly cannot serve as true utterance of the latter's union with the intellect. Rather, says Newman, it is the image which perpetuates the thing itself. St. Thomas would probably call that image a phantasm—the sense impression on which the agent intellect works to abstract the intelligible species. Clearly therefore he would reverse Newman's proposition and insist that it is by the notion, not the image, that we "take hold of objects from within them" and thereby truly *perpetuate* them. After all, it is the notion which expresses the intellect's penetration into the individual and the soul's union with the intelligible form, which is the principle of that individual's being. The image (phantasm) gives us only the raw material of intellection—the fact of an individual's existence, not an apprehension of its very being. Therefore St. Thomas would no doubt say that it is the image, if we rest in it as the end of the cognitive process, which *transforms* the thing, because it provides merely a reflection of the thing, not the thing itself. The notion alone is capable of giving us the *res* in its proper nature.

Newman consistently takes the contrary view. He speaks, for instance, in his *Discourses on University Education* of a "circle of sciences" and of a "circle of objects" which the former reflects. However, he does not say—in fact he explicitly denies—that the former, being conceptual, conveys as knowledge the very being of the latter. The sciences, he says, "are but aspects of things; they are severally incomplete in their relation to the things themselves, though complete in their own idea and for their own respective purposes." It necessarily follows that the whole circle of the sciences is incomplete in relationship to the circle of objects it reflects. "Viewed altogether," the sciences "approximate to a representation or subjective reflection of the objective truth, as nearly as is possible to the human mind," but that "nearly as possible" is never complete. Indeed the sciences, "as being abstractions, have far more to do with the relations of things than with things themselves." In fact the sciences, at best, can "never tell us all that can be said about a thing, even when they tell something, nor do they bring it before us, *as the senses do*"[10] (italics added).

These statements clearly anticipate the disparagement of notions which is stated so fully in the *Grammar of Assent* seventeen years later. Moreover, the last clause here quoted, "as the senses do," anticipates Newman's later espousal of real apprehensions; for really to apprehend something is to grasp it sensibly and imaginatively. The very word *apprehension* is indicative of the direction in which Newman's thought is moving, for it might be regarded as a tacit admission that he seeks something other than knowledge or science as a mode of cognition. For one thing, *apprehension* is as vague as *knowledge* is exact; and since the mode of cognition Newman wishes to signify defies exact definition, that very vagueness is an advantage to him. When one apprehends something, he somehow grasps or perceives it, and to define the *somehow* with precision would be to return to classical and Scholastic distinctions between sensation and intellection, images and notions. Perhaps the best way to understand real apprehension is to say that it bears close resemblance to the modern use of the word *intuition.* In Scholastic philosophy intuition is strictly intellectual; indeed it is the property of purely intellectual beings —the Holy Angels and the demons. Insofar as it applies to men it is identified with the *intellectus* and is understood to signify the immediate understanding of self-evident intellectual propositions. As such it is clearly seen to be a constituent of conceptual knowledge—a source of premises from which the *ratio* proceeds to its conclusions. However, in modern usage, intuition has come to signify a substitution of feeling and imagination for intellection, of sensation and image for idea, and that, of course, is virtually the same substitution which Newman effects when he replaces *knowledge* or *science* with *apprehension.* When Kant says that "all our intuition takes place by means of the senses alone," he is, in effect, substituting intuition for conception. As radically as Newman may disagree with Kant and his other fellow moderns in matters of dogma, he joins them in their retreat from a traditional belief in the efficacy of knowledge in its fully conceptual sense.

The reason for that retreat is fully understandable, and we can see the logic of it from the evidence which we now have before us. If the concept transforms and distorts the thing of which it is the concept, it only makes sense to attempt some other, truer mode of apprehending it. If St. Thomas had believed, as Newman did, that the notion was merely a dilution and starvation of the thing it represented, he too, no doubt, would have abandoned notions. Newman and Aquinas both seek the real; the difference between them lies in their divergent estimates of how the real can be seized. I know of no evidence that Newman ever made a careful study of St. Thomas's theory of intellection or passed judgment on it. However, it is interesting to consider the possibility that had he been persuaded that the Angelic Doctor was correct in his teaching—that the concept utters the real, the very being of the *res*—he might have espoused rather than rejected Thomist epistemology. (And Newman's theory of cognition does amount to such a rejection, albeit tacit.) One can only wish, for the sake of modern Catholic theology and poetry, that that condition contrary to fact had in fact obtained; for without concepts—without knowledge—there can be no legitimate metaphysics, no valid approach to God by the exercise of the unaided natural reason.

That impossibility is proved in the event by Newman's statements concerning an apprehension of God independent of Revelation. He maintains that such an apprehension is possible, but when we examine his "Proof of Theism," we shall see how widely his thesis diverges from St. Thomas's. For the latter a natural theology is the fruit of metaphysics; the intellect is the agency thereof. For Newman, natural theology is a consequence of ethical perceptions and is the work of the conscience. Aquinas surveys the visible creation and through the exercise of reason derives a knowledge of God from it. Newman looks into the "living busy world" and sees no reflection of its Creator; were it not, he says, for the voice of God speaking "in my conscience and my heart, I should be an atheist, or a pantheist, or a polytheist when I looked into the world."[11]

Newman argues that a proof of God's existence derived from the perceptions of the conscience satisfies the Church's requirement that he believe God accessible to demonstration as well as to faith. He insists, for instance, that our apprehension of God through His manifestation to the conscience is inseparable from our apprehension of our own being. We do not require faith in that apprehension; rather, since it is an experience, we take it as self-evident. That is what he means in the *Apologia* when he says that "the being of a God . . . is as certain to me as the certainty of my own existence" (p. 216); and since "it would be improper to say that I *believe* in my being, or make an act of foi aveugle in my being,"[12] it would likewise be improper to say that one believes in God as He presents Himself to the conscience. Therefore Newman feels perfectly justified in constructing a theory of "natural religion" on the dictates of conscience (*Grammar*, pp. 295–310), and we must grant that such a religion may be defined legitimately as natural in distinction from revealed religion.

However, it is one thing to speak of natural religion in a general sense and quite another to speak of a natural *knowledge* of God's existence, and the question which presents itself is whether the perceptions of conscience can, by any stretch of the imagination, be called knowledge. We are constrained to answer in the negative, for Newman's proof of theism does not give us concepts or understanding of God. Newman as much as acknowledges that fact when he speaks of perceiving things "prior to faith" by "intuition." He grasps the fact of his own existence, the fact of conscience, and the fact of God which conscience manifests by what he describes as "one complex act of intuition" (*Notebook*, p. 71). So widely divergent is that intuition from knowledge in the usual sense of the term that, as he tells us in the *Apologia*, there is great difficulty in translating its "certainty into logical shape" (p. 216). We might legitimately read *intuition* as *real apprehension,* for the proof of God from the conscience is, when all is said and done, a substitution of real apprehension for notional in the traditional territory of metaphysics. Moreover it may be worth recalling that that substitution was not original with Newman. As Gilson remarks, with specific reference to Kant, moralism is "one of the classical escapes from scepticism for those who despair of philosophy."[13]

III

That Newman did despair of philosophy, that he had no metaphysics in the traditional sense of the term, seems an inescapable conclusion from the evidence before us. An appeal to the sort of experience which Kant calls intuition and Newman real apprehension cannot suffice for a genuine knowledge of things whether visible or invisible; and the consequence of that insufficiency is to place Newman in a rather curious position with reference to the history of western thought.

We have seen how he differs from Aquinas; with whom, if anyone, does he agree? One is tempted to answer (as Przywara, for instance, does) that he is to be identified in terms of the Platonist-Augustinian tradition.[14] Certainly we may speak of Newman's Augustinian interiority, and there are several passages in his work in which he speaks in Platonist or neo-Platonist fashion of the physical creation's being "but the manifestation to our senses of realities greater than itself" (*Ap.*, p. 36). Indeed Newman's whole theory of the visible world as an economy or symbol of the invisible might be construed in Platonist terms, and certainly that view of creation stands in radical contradiction to Aquinas's. On the other hand we cannot say that Newman was a Platonist or an Augustinian in any very precise sense; for the necessary corollary of a belief in the visible creation's being a symbol of the invisible and also of the appeal to interior experience (as to the memory) for knowledge of God, is a doctrine of innate or infused species. Whatever their differences may be, Platonists and Augustinians agree with Thomists that the intellect must have access to intelligible species in order to *know*. If the intellect does not abstract those species from composite substances, it must obtain them in some other fashion—by participating them innately or, in St. Augustine's teaching, by their being directly infused by God into the soul. Without infused species Augustine's withdrawal into the intellect for the knowledge of God makes no sense whatever; without innate species the Platonist has no means of apprehending the invisible things

which lie behind the veil of the physical creation and hence
no key to understanding what the *visibilia* signify. Yet New-
man, who withdraws for an apprehension of God into the re-
cesses of the self and who perceives the creation as an econ-
omy, specifically denies belief in innate species (*Notebook,*
p. 25).

The fact of the matter is that Newman does not really be-
lieve in knowledge on any level; and whenever the species
fecundates the intellect—however that species be conceived
as entering the soul—knowledge, conceptual statement of
truth, is the consequence. Therefore, though Newman may re-
semble the Platonists and Augustinians more closely than the
Thomists, we must finally conclude that he diverges from them
radically in regard to the central issue of the possibility of
metaphysical wisdom. Curiously enough Newman's position is
similar to the teaching of Democritus which St. Thomas cites
and rejects: "Democritus and the other early philosophers did
not distinguish between intellect and sense," whereas both
the Platonists and Aristotelians, whatever their differences
subsequent to that distinction, agree to that rudimentary
premise. Because Democritus did not agree, he "held that *all
knowledge is caused by images issuing from the bodies we
think of and entering into our souls,*" and we see immediately
how closely this theory of knowledge "caused by a *discharge
of images*" (*ST,* I, 84, 6) resembles real apprehension or the
modern sense of intuition. In this connection we must not for-
get Newman's cardinal premise that it is "the whole man" who
reasons—not the intellect by itself but the entire composite of
thought, feeling, and even action which we signify by the
word *man.* Such a proposition suggests, much as Democritus's
philosophy does, that there is finally no more than a nominal
distinction between intellect and sense, and from such con-
siderations we begin to see how profound Newman's anti-
intellectualism, his divergence from all traditional metaphysics,
is. Sceptical of the intelligibility of the material creation,
sceptical of the intellect's power to acquire species by abstrac-
tion, sceptical of the doctrines of innate or infused species, he

is confined, for cognition, whether of creatures or of Creator, to a doctrine of instinctive or intuitive apprehension which is, historically speaking, primitive and which therefore requires him to confuse the basic distinction between sense and intellect on which all classical western thought is based. In short his scepticism places him, philosophically if not doctrinally, in the camp of Blake and the Romantics, of Yeats and the moderns, whose possession and keen delight is restricted to the rattle of pebbles in the Faith's recession and the great song's silence. Yet Newman is the chief theological influence on the Catholic Church in which Hopkins and Eliot wrote.

3
Newman and Aquinas: Theology

NEWMAN'S distrust of conceptual reason not only deprives him of a legitimate metaphysics; it also impairs his theology. To understand how that is so we must see how he differs from Aquinas and Dante in his teachings concerning the virtue of faith.

Theology is a science of divine things, and faith is the source of that science's first principles. It can be taken as axiomatic that there can be no adequate access to supernatural things save by supernatural means, and faith, according to Catholic theology, is that means. What a man cannot apprehend by his senses and his reason he must acquire in some other way, and that way is by believing in what has been revealed to him by God. Given the nature of the human intellect and its dependence on sense experience for the raw material on which it works, there is simply no means, save by believing what is revealed, whereby man may have knowledge of God—except, of course, that limited knowledge of God's existence and of His nature as cause, sustainer, and mover of the cosmos to which natural or metaphysical wisdom may attain. Nor, save faith, is there any means—even the exercise of natural reason—whereby a science of divine things can be held with such sureness, with such freedom from doubt, that the subject of belief is as certain to the mind as those material creatures which the senses apprehend.

To propositions such as these all orthodox Christians would assent. However, just as we have seen that two wholly orthodox churchmen, Aquinas and Newman, on account of radical differences in convictions and in historical circumstances, place different emphases on the doctrine of a natural knowledge of

God, so we shall find that the same men place different emphases on the orthodox Christian conception of faith. Moreover, just as St. Thomas's conception of the human intellect and its capacity is far more liberal and more spacious than Newman's, allowing for an orderly and luminous vision of the cosmos such as that which we encounter in Dante's poetry, so too we shall find that St. Thomas's teachings concerning faith are also more nearly susceptible than Newman's to metaphysical and metaphoric elaboration.

Let us consider these differences in detail, recalling at the outset that faith is a theological virtue. That means, as St. Thomas says, that unlike all other virtues (except, of course, hope and charity) faith is not in our nature, according either to "aptitude" or "inchoation," but "entirely from without" (*ST,* II [1], 63, 1). On this matter, again, all orthodox Christians, whatever their epistemological differences, would agree. Man does not summon faith from the recesses of his nature; God gives it to him. However, that does not mean that faith contradicts nature; and it is on this point that Newman departs, in emphasis if not in fact, from Aquinas. It is important to keep the distinction between emphasis and fact in view, for Newman never teaches such a contradiction in explicit terms. He even speaks of, insists upon, the harmony of the two. Nevertheless, as we shall now see, the tendency of his thought on the whole is toward such a contradiction, and that tendency is germane to all the differences which separate him from St. Thomas. The latter, both in explicit doctrine and implicit emphasis, makes it perfectly clear that the relationship between the theological virtues and man's nature is simply a specific instance of the general rule that grace is given to perfect, not to destroy nature. Faith is not natural—it does not reside in human nature—but when it is bestowed by God on that nature, it does not contradict or weaken it; rather it serves to enrich, enhance, and complete it.

In particular, faith perfects the intellect; and Victorian and modern scepticism notwithstanding, so far from there being an inherent opposition between faith and reason, there is, according to St. Thomas, a perfect concord. That concord stems from the fact that man was created to live in a state of grace. His failure to do so is a consequence of his original sin, not of his nature. He was created to be a receptacle for grace, and that means, among other things, that his will and intellect are so ordered that they fulfill themselves by responding to charity, faith, and hope. These virtues are not by nature in the intellect and will, but the intellect and will are, by nature, incomplete without them; in much the same way that a fireplace is incomplete without a fire or a decanter without brandy, and yet the fire and the spirits are "entirely from without." Thus the theological virtues, though thoroughly supernatural, both in respect to their source and to the end of their operation, are in no sense against nature; for man is made for supernatural happiness, and to that end he requires the infusion of theological virtues. Thus St. Thomas teaches that "it is by faith that the intellect apprehends the object of hope and love" (*ST,* II [1], 62, 4), which object, of course, is God, for whom man's nature was made. In this regard one recalls how careful Dante is to show that man's form, his being, his nature, is perfected by supernatural grace, specifically by faith, hope and charity, and that the best analogy for man's freedom in grace is the freedom of fire and water to move according to their form or nature.

Once we understand fully that faith and reason work in harmony rather than in opposition, we are in a position to understand what St. Paul means when he defines faith as "the substance of things hoped for, the evidence of things not seen." Aquinas's analysis of the definition rests on the two words *substance* and *evidence.* The former, as St. Paul uses it, "does not stand for the supreme genus condivided with the other genera, but for that *likeness to substance which is found in each genus, inasmuch as the first thing in a genus contains the others virtually and is said to be the substance thereof"* (*ST,* II [2], 4, 1; italics added). Faith, according to Aquinas, is just such a "first thing" in reference to the whole body of "things hoped for"; it "contains the others virtually and is

said to be the substance thereof." Those "things to be hoped
for" are ultimately subsumed in one thing, the "First Truth,"
which is the proper object of the intellect. Moreover that
"First Truth" is, by definition, "unseen," therefore unpossessed,
at least in its fullness, and therefore yet to be hoped for. Thus
to speak of possessing the "first thing" which "contains the
others virtually" when those others are, really, *that* other, the
unseen "First Truth," is really to speak of possessing God.
Hence we see that to define faith as the "substance of things
hoped for" is to say that faith is the beginning of the knowl-
edge of God which contains the fullness of such knowledge
virtually; that it is the seed, indeed the mustard seed, from
which the great tree grows and which contains the great tree,
virtually, in its small compass. In short we might say that St.
Paul's definition, as Aquinas interprets it, is a paradox of the
same sort which our Lord used constantly in his teaching,
which poets have also used in all ages, and which is necessary
for the statement of divine mysteries. Faith is the present pos-
session of what we do not yet have; the immediate knowledge
of the "First Truth" which we cannot yet know. The image of
the seed and the recognition that it contains the tree virtually,
or the explanation that substance is the "first thing" which
contains the others virtually—these formulae elucidate the
paradox, but they do not exhaust its mystery. That mystery is
enriched and compounded when we remember that faith,
though supernatural and "entirely from without," is neverthe-
less "in the intellect" and is given to man to perfect the intel-
lect. For the consequence of the two teachings in conjunction
is that by faith man's intellect attains to what it cannot attain
to—the impossible but available knowledge of God.

   Dante gives essentially the same definition. In the twenty-
fourth canto of the "Paradiso" St. Peter commands him to
speak and declare what faith is. Dante replies, as we would
expect him to, with St. Paul's definition:

> *fede è sustanza di cose sperate,*
> *ed argomento delle non parventi;*
> *e questa pare a me sua quiditate.*   (*Par.,* xxiv, 64–66)

(Faith is the substance of things hoped for and the
evidence of things not seen; and this I take to be its
quiddity.)

St. Peter responds by saying in effect, so far, so good, but why
does St. Paul place faith first "among the substances and after
among the evidences"? (*Par.,* xxiv, 67–69). Dante's answer,
with regard to substance, might be regarded as a restatement of
Aquinas's definition in which some of the technical distinctions
are muted and the mystery of the paradox thereby heightened:

> *E io appresso: 'Le profonde cose*
> *che mi largiscon qui la lor parvenza,*
> *alli occhi di là giù son sì ascose,*
> *che l'esser loro v'è in sola credenza,*
> *sopra la qual si fonda l'alta spene;*
> *e però di sustanza prende intenza.'* (*Par.,* xxiv, 70–75)

(And I then: "The deep things which so richly mani-
fest themselves to me here are so hidden from men's
eyes below that there their existence lies in belief alone,
on which is based the lofty hope; and therefore it
takes the character of substance.")

If I understand Dante's statement correctly, he is saying, as
Aquinas is, that faith is a substance in the sense that it is the
foundation upon which all that we hope for is built, the seed
from which what we hope for grows. The way in which he
phrases his explanation places a heavy emphasis on the fact
that faith is a means by which man possesses divine things on
earth. In that sense, too, it is a substance: the real though,
paradoxically, impossible existence of heavenly things in mortal
vessels. That which Dante sees clearly in heaven is so hidden
from men's eyes below *that there their existence lies in belief
alone* (*che l'esser loro v'e in sola credenza*). Indeed it is only
in *sola credenza* that heavenly things have substance or ex-
istence in this world. Faith according to these explanations is
the real presence of the knowledge of God, now in the time of
this mortal life; it gives things hoped for, which are the whole
of divine truth, a substantial existence here below.

The same understanding of faith is made even clearer in St. Thomas's explanation of St. Paul's term *evidence*—the "evidence of things not seen." *Evidence,* says St. Thomas, "is taken for the result of evidence" in the same way that *substance* is taken to signify "the first beginnings" of things hoped for. "For evidence induces the intellect to adhere to a truth, wherefore the firm adhesion of the intellect to the nonapparent truth of faith is called *evidence* here" (*ST,* II [2], 4, I). St. Thomas's actual word is *argumentum,* which makes the meaning still clearer; for *argumentum* suggests not only evidence in the usual English sense but also the idea of persuasion or conviction. We might say, therefore, that it is "persuasive evidence" or "evidence sufficient for conviction" which "induces the intellect to adhere to a truth" and that faith is just such a virtue whose object is supernatural truth or the "First Truth." Thus Aquinas points out that "another reading has *conviction,* because, to wit, the intellect of the believer is convinced by Divine authority, so as to assent to what it sees not" (*ST,* II [2], 4, I). That assent, as we have seen, makes the invisible present and, in some sense, even visible to the intellect. Therefore we see that the evidence or *argumentum* of "things not seen" has the same paradoxical power as "the substance of things hoped for." In either case St. Paul is saying that faith, because it is a theological virtue, unites the human intellect to a divine knowledge which, though it completes or perfects the intellect, is by nature impossible for it. Thus faith unites heaven with earth and gives, if we may borrow the metaphor, "a local habitation" to those divine realities which in themselves are bounded by nothing but rather are the boundary and habitation of all things.

II

To turn in our consideration of faith from Aquinas and Dante to Newman is, as we might expect, to shift our attention from modes of knowledge to modes of apprehension and intuition. Again we must stress the fact that the difference is one of emphasis, for Newman never directly contradicts St. Thomas's doctrine concerning faith. However, he places a different construction upon that doctrine, and the difference has profound consequences for Christian theology and poetry. Newman, like Aquinas, teaches that man must hold the supernatural reality by faith and by faith only; but the way in which he interprets that holding limits the scope of what can be held. The limitation is the consequence of the same distrust of concepts and the same reliance, instead of concepts, on sensations and images, which deprive Newman of a legitimate metaphysics. It is important in this regard to remember that in Aquinas's teaching sensation and image are excluded by the specification that "faith resides in the intellect" rather than in the will and affections.

Let us consider first the affective emphasis of Newman's teaching. It is possible to come at the matter from any one of several directions and in any one of several works; but perhaps the clearest statement of it is in the tenth and eleventh of the *Oxford University Sermons,* "Faith and Reason, Contrasted as Habits of Mind" and "The Nature of Faith in Relation to Reason." Both of these were preached in 1839, but in the *Grammar of Assent* thirty years later we find that Newman's basic principles are unchanged; and the "simplicity" of the *University Sermons* relative to the *Grammar* gives them the character of a lucid introduction to the principles of the later work.

On the rudimentary relationship between faith and reason Newman is wholly orthodox and wholly within the Patristic and Scholastic tradition of interpretation. St. Augustine learned from the apostles and the fathers that the invisible things of God, though manifest in some measure in the things that are made, can only be known in their fullness by faith—that reason cannot attain to them. He gave that principle its classic formulation: *credo ut intelligam.* I do not reason and understand in order that I may believe; rather I believe in order that I may understand. Faith furnishes the premises upon which a legitimate exercise of reason on divine matters must rest; conversely no amount of understanding divine matters can lead to faith. Upon this distinction, upon *credo ut intelligam,* the whole edifice of medieval theology is founded; and as we have just seen, Aquinas is in this matter in full accord with Augustine and with the fathers. Faith is a theological virtue and "entirely from without." Newman teaches the same thing: "Faith is an instrument of knowledge and action, unknown to the world before, a principle *sui generis,* distinct from those which nature supplies, and in particular (which is the point into which I mean to inquire) independent of what is commonly understood by Reason." In the qualifying footnote, added in the uniform edition, Newman resolves any doubt as to what he means by Reason as it is "commonly understood." It is "the habit of deciding about religious questions with the off-hand random judgments which are suggested by secular principles. . . . At best, by Reason is usually meant, the faculty of Reason exercising itself explicitly by *a posteriori* or evidential methods." Faith according to Newman is other than, prior to, such reasoning; for "if, after all, it turns out merely to be a believing upon evidence, or a sort of conclusion upon a process of reasoning, a resolve formed upon a calculation, the inspired text is not level to the understanding."[1] Augustine, Aquinas, Dante, and all orthodox Christians must agree.

However, upon that traditional foundation of familiar principles Newman proceeds to erect a modern and unfamiliar argument. It depends from his statement that one central distinction between reason and faith is that the latter is "content with weaker evidence" than the former (*Sermons,* p. 185), a fact which causes worldly men to regard faith as merely superstition. The matter of "weaker evidence" is not in itself unique or novel in Newman's case; St. Thomas acknowledges the same distinction between faith and reason, pointing out that though man cannot trace the content of faith "back to first principles, by which all our judgments are guided" (*ST,* II [2], 2, 3), there is nevertheless no danger in believing so to speak on "weak evidence," because the virtue of faith serves in lieu of the natural light of intellect by which we normally assent to first principles. Faith itself is the "evidence of things not seen." For Aquinas the matter is worth no more than a single objection and reply, for the resolution of the problem is implicit in his whole teaching that faith, though "entirely from without," perfects rather than contradicts the intellect. For Newman, however, the distinction between faith and reason in regard to strength of evidence is a matter of capital importance, for it involves the question of faith's validity in a scientifically oriented and secular age. In responding to the charge that faith is indistinguishable from superstition Newman is constrained to show why it is "reasonable" to believe divine things on the basis of weaker evidence than that which we demand for human things. It is little exaggeration to say that that constraint informs all of his writing on faith and reason and that his response to the challenge of a secular age, though it secures orthodoxy, distorts the traditional emphasis of that orthodoxy.

The reason for that distortion is that Newman accepts too many of his adversaries' assumptions and is too nearly persuaded that their secular use of reason is an inevitable consequence of that faculty's exercise. Though he assents to the proposition that faith and reason work in concord with one another, that grace is given to perfect rather than to destroy nature, he is constantly betraying presuppositions (possibly only half-conscious ones) to the contrary. For instance, he remarks that "when the Gospel is said to require a rational Faith, this need not mean more than that Faith is accordant to right Reason in the abstract, not that it results from it in the particular case" (*Sermons*, p. 184). The question is whether Newman's qualification does not amount in effect to a negation of the Thomist principle of concord between faith and reason. That "Faith is accordant to right Reason in the abstract" may not mean that it is ever accordant to it "in the particular case"; and, if not, the concord between the two may have no more than a nominal existence. That that is the case is suggested by the fact that Newman seems to accept a secular interpretation of reason at its face value; that he grants the scientists and other modern sceptics their atheistic conclusions as the inevitable consequence of rational investigation and turns to the "weaker evidence" of faith, not as the perfection of reason, but as an alternative to it.

Consider his remarks on Gibbon's scepticism: "when a well-known infidel of the last century argues, that the divinity of Christianity is founded on the testimony of the Apostles, in opposition to the experience of nature, and that the laws of nature are uniform, those of testimony variable, and scoffingly adds that Christianity is founded on Faith, not on Reason, what is this but saying that Reason is severer in its demands of evidence than Faith?" (*Sermons*, p. 185). What indeed! But the question is whether Gibbon's view of nature and of reason is correct. Newman, in any event, assents to that view. Indeed he seems to feel that he must answer Gibbon and his sort on their own grounds, by admitting their premises: that the "laws of nature" as reason apprehends them are "uniform" and therefore exclude the miraculous; that to hold the Christian religion we must appeal from reason to faith, not as from a lower to a higher tribunal or from things partial to things complete, but rather as from one pole of experience to its opposite—poles of experience which may not be contradictory "in the abstract" but which invariably seem to be "in the particular case."

We are now in a position to see how strikingly Newman's emphasis differs from that of Aquinas and Dante—so strikingly in fact that though they teach identical doctrines the effect of their respective emphases causes the identical teachings to issue in radically different views of the Christian religion. How, for instance, would Aquinas respond to "a well-known infidel of the last century"? The question is necessarily hypothetical, but it is not difficult to see how the principles of the *Summa* furnish an answer to Gibbon which is ultimately more satisfactory than Newman's. Aquinas would simply accuse Gibbon of begging the question, of assuming, without proving it, that the laws of nature exclude the possibility of miraculous intervention and that reason properly exercised apprehends a secular view of creation. He would argue, on the contrary, that the so-called "laws of nature," by which both Gibbon and Newman mean the laws of the physical creation, are part of a vast system of law which descends in hierarchical order from the *lex eterna,* which is the very mind of God Himself; that because they have both a common source and a hierarchical relationship to one another it is impossible for the various types of law within this system to contradict one another; and that therefore what may appear to be a miraculous violation of the "laws of nature," of the physical system, by the divine law (which is the law of miraculous intervention) is no more than apparent. Rather the higher is joined to the lower, the divine to the physical, in terms of the original harmony which God ordained in the creation. Since man's reason is also created by the same God who made the physical universe and gave it its laws, and since reason is so constituted that it relies upon the senses for its raw material and therefore proceeds in its inquiry from the physical world which the senses apprehend, it is impossible that reason, if rightly exercised, can come to secular conclusions about the universe. Indeed the fact of metaphysical wisdom, of a natural knowledge of God derived from a knowledge of the creature, indicates that the reason, when properly exercised, ascends the great chain of being, perceiving in the *visibilia* the "invisible things of God." In other words Aquinas would argue that Gibbon and other such modern seculars—and Newman to the extent that he accepts their premises—have used their reason improperly. Their secular conclusion, their persuasion that reason demonstrates a uniform nature which is hostile to miraculous intervention, proves that misuse beyond question. They have argued that a creation whose very existence is dependent on God at every point in time and space, a creation which is so ordered by God, through laws, that "all which revolves in mind and space" gives the taste of Him, a creation whose divine principle of being is accessible to the human intellect, is a mere mechanism, describable only by a sceptical science, the contemplation of which leads to atheism. Newman did not *believe* that; however, he seems to be persuaded that reason, as it is exercised "in the particular case," leads to that conclusion. Consequently he must rely almost wholly on belief.

Let us draw these various strands of argument together. We have seen already that Newman's distrust of concepts is the consequence of his scepticism about the capacity of the intellect to enter into a real union with the form of the thing known. The appeal from knowledge to apprehension which results from that distrust of concepts deprives him of a legitimate metaphysics—of a knowledge of God drawn from a knowledge of the *visibilia.* That inability to understand God's "innermost presence" in His works leads in turn to the conviction that reason necessarily reaches secular conclusions about those works, that the creation when contemplated by conceptual intellect shows no reflection of its Creator. Hence for a natural (as opposed to a revealed) knowledge of God, one must appeal not to the notional reason but to that particular form of real apprehension or intuition known as the conscience. However, such an appeal, though it may constitute a legitimate "proof of theism," in no way helps us to see God in His works or to understand that the divine law is perfectly concordant with the laws of the physical creation, the miraculous with the natural. When faith comes to tell us that God is really present in His works and that miracles are really not contrary to nature and therefore not "impossible," in order to make its proclamation it must necessarily contradict the conclusions of the conceptual reason. Hypothetically, "in the abstract," faith and reason are harmonious: reason ought not to present us with a secular view of things. However, "in the particular case," because reason must depend for its operation on notions which starve and dilute the real, it goes astray. Therefore in order to correct reason, faith must in some large measure contradict it, and it does so by replacing reason's reasons (if we may use such a phrase) by its own "weaker reasons." As we shall now see, these latter are weak in the very way we might expect, in being less purely notional, more intuitive, more nearly dependent on ethical apprehensions than the former are.

On the other hand it is easy to see, from St. Thomas's point of view, how faith can perfect reason without contradicting it or without substituting weak reasons for valid concepts. If reason, unaided, can prove God's existence and if concepts can give us valid knowledge of Him as the *ipsum esse,* the uncaused cause, the source of all created being, faith's task obviously will not be to contradict the reason but to supplement it. In short, if one begins with a valid metaphysical knowledge of God, the task of theology will be to enrich or complete rather than to displace or contradict the discernments of reason. Newman's failure in regard to metaphysics (it is ultimately, I suppose, his failure to understand that the concept conveys the truth of the *res extra animam*) and his consequent predisposition to accept the assumptions about nature and reason which characterize modern atheism, necessitates his subsequent appeal to "previous notices, prepossessions, and (in a good sense of the word) prejudices," as necessary antecedents to the act of faith (*Sermons,* p. 187). It is these antecedents which weaken faith's reasons and which introduce a consideration of the affections into a definition of assent.

Newman's argument proceeds as follows: since reason, using strong evidence, comes to secular conclusions and since faith, using weak evidence, comes to religious conclusions, how can we justify faith against the charge of scepticism and how can we rest with certitude on its supernatural object? In other words, unless we are to dismiss reason altogether and become pure fideists (and Newman never goes that far), "how is it conformable to Reason to accept evidence less than Reason requires? If Faith be what has been described, it opposes itself to Reason, as being satisfied with the less where Reason demands the more. If, then, Reason be the healthy action of the mind, then Faith must be its weakness." Why is that not the case? "For this reason, because it [Faith] is mainly swayed by antecedent considerations," by "previous notices, prepossessions, and . . . prejudices"; because "the mind that believes is acted upon by its own hopes, fears, and existing opinions," and because those "antecedent considerations" have a legitimate place in the act of belief (*Sermons,* pp. 187–88). Anyone who is familiar with Newman's work knows that this appeal to "antecedent considerations" which touch the heart is a central motif throughout his canon. It is a consequence, of course, of his preference of apprehension and intuition to knowledge, and it manifests itself in all his arguments about the cogency of belief—primarily in his distinction between implicit and explicit reason, in his thesis that the whole man reasons, and in his doctrine of the illative sense.[2] I do not intend at the moment to examine those various manifestations of the thesis but rather to consider its epistemological ramifications.

We have called Newman's theory of faith "affective," and that term must now be stressed. By it I mean more than a simple appeal to the feelings, for one cannot say that Newman merely identifies faith with feeling in opposition to reason. In fact he denies such an identification on several occasions. On the other hand those "antecedent considerations" to which Newman appeals, those "hopes, fears and existing opinions," are functions of the imagination and the feelings, even perhaps of the will, rather than of the intellect. It would be more accurate still to say that they belong to "the whole man," to the complex of sensations, memory, imagination, will, and reason, rather than to reason alone. Such a statement of the case does full justice to Newman's thesis, and it in no way suggests that that thesis leans more heavily on the emotions than it in fact does. On the other hand it leaves no doubt either (and this is the crucial point) that Newman conceives the intellect as being moved to faith by those powers of the soul which we normally consider to be "affective" rather than rational or intelligent.

St. Thomas's teaching provides an interesting contrast to Newman's, for he insists much more strongly than Newman does on the intellectual primacy of the act of faith. He does not deny that the will (and, through the will, the affections) is involved in belief, but he does insist that belief itself is in the intellect; and that is necessarily the case because the object of faith is not the good but *"the true,* which pertains properly to the intellect." When Augustine said that *"faith resides in the believer's will,"* he was taking "faith for the act of faith . . . in so far as [the] intellect assents to matters of faith at the command of the will." Aquinas is quick to admit that "the intellect needs to be well disposed to follow the command of the will" (*ST,* II [2], 4, 2; italics in original: St. Thomas is quoting Augustine). However, it is clear that that which commands is distinct from that which is commanded and that though the will may direct the intellect to believe, the will does not believe. The intellect believes, the will loves; faith belongs to the intellect, charity to the will. Though the two virtues are inseparable in their activity, their natures are as clearly distinct as the powers of the soul into which they are infused.

Newman does not deny that distinction; he remains, as always, technically correct in his theological statements. However, though he does not deny that belief is in the intellect rather than in the will or affections, he blurs the distinctions between them in such a fashion as to diminish the importance of the intellect's proper act. Consider his interpretation of the Scholastic distinction (which he learned not directly from the Schoolmen but from the Caroline divines) between *fides formata charitate* and *fides formata ratione.* The former is living or "justifying" faith, the latter a "dead faith, which an infidel may have; so that which justifies or is acceptable in God's sight, lives in, and from, a desire after those things which it accepts and confesses" (*Sermons,* p. 193). On its face this argument is perfectly valid by Thomist standards. Aquinas also distinguishes between a living and a lifeless faith, and the basis of the distinction is the presence or absence of charity. "Charity is called the form of faith because it quickens the act of faith" (*ST,* II [2], 4, 3). The word "quickens" means "to make alive," and form, as we have already discovered, is that which gives life and being. Therefore, since charity is, in one sense, the form of faith, faith without charity is dead. However, we must note the phrase "in one sense," for charity is not faith's only form or its only source of life. In fact, because charity is in the will and faith in the intellect, it is impossible that charity should be the form of faith in the sense that "a form and the thing of which it is the form are in one subject . . . [and] form one simply" (*ST,* II [2], 4, 3). In other words charity is not the "intrinsic form" of faith; it does not give faith its being. Rather it is called the form of living or justifying faith almost in a metaphoric sense, in that it quickens faith, as we have said.

These distinctions are very important for our purposes, for they indicate, again, the difference in emphasis which separates Newman from Aquinas. Both agree to the distinction between living and lifeless faith, but whereas Newman virtually identifies the former simply as faith and eliminates the latter (virtually but, again, not literally), the effect of Aquinas's argument is to show that "living and lifeless faith are one and the same habit," that with or without charity faith remains, for "faith is a perfection of the intellect" and what "pertains *directly* to faith . . . pertains to the intellect" (*ST,* II [2], 4, 4; italics added). In other words, though without the motivation of charity in the will faith is fruitless and ineffectual for salvation, faith, in itself, does not depend for its being on any power of the soul other than the intellect. Newman always speaks as though it is impossible for the intellect to assent to God unless it is motivated to that assent by will and desire. "It is indeed a great question whether Atheism is not as philosophically consistent with the phenomena of the physical world, taken by themselves, as the doctrine of a creative and governing Power" (*Sermons,* p. 194). Therefore for the intellect to assent to the existence of such a power it must be moved to do so by man's "love for it, his love being strong, though the testimony is weak" (*Sermons,* p. 203). "But love of the great Object of Faith, watchful attention to Him, readiness to believe Him near, easiness to believe Him interposing in human affairs, fear of the risk of slighting or missing what may really come from Him; . . . these are the feelings which make us think evidence sufficient, which falls short of a proof in itself" (*Sermons*, p. 193).

This emphasis on the affections as conducive to faith is seen most clearly in Newman's interpretation of St. Paul's definition. He intimates that when St. Paul speaks of the "substance of things hoped for," he means that it is the hoping itself which makes that substantial presence of those things possible. He interprets the Apostle to be saying that faith "is the reckoning that to be, which it hopes or wishes to be"; and with reference to the phrase "evidence of things not seen," Newman's comment is that faith's "desire is its main evidence" (*Sermons*, p. 190). Newman even goes so far as to translate *substance* with his favorite word, *realizing*—suggesting thereby that what St. Paul really means is that faith is the making real in terms of the feelings and desires of the believer (for realization, which is a cognate of real apprehension or intuition, belongs to "the whole man") precisely what the believer has already felt and desired. Though in formal theological statement Newman always insists that faith is a theological virtue, subjected in the intellect, there can be little question that such statements as these lead him away from that precise definition in an affective and subjective direction. Certainly the word *substance* cannot be translated as *realizing* unless one is prepared to say that faith makes present, not God Himself *as known,* but rather an apprehension of Him as he is reflected in our affective faculties. It is interesting, too, that when he speaks of faith specifically as a theological virtue, he defines it, not as a "supernaturally implanted knowledge" but rather as a "supernaturally implanted *instinct*",[3] and instinct belongs, of course, to the affection rather than to the reason, to the world of intuition rather than of concept.

In other words, when Newman speaks of *fides formata charitate,* he really means that the affective faculties of the soul, overwhelming the incurably secular bent of the conceptual reason, move the intellect to believe and thus make faith possible. For Aquinas, on the contrary, that which makes faith possible, its "intrinsic form," is a habit or disposition of the intellect itself; and because "faith resides in the intellect," it is logically impossible for faith to be made possible by the will or the desires. Newman, on the other hand, says un-equivocally that what is finally established in the reason is "begun in the will."[4] Moreover, even when Aquinas speaks of charity in the will as the form of a justifying faith, he still differs from Newman in an important respect; for he makes a sharper distinction than Newman does between the will and the feelings or desires. Charity as an act of will may involve feeling, but feeling is not its form or source. Thus, if we speak in Thomist terms, to say that charity "quickens faith" is not in any sense to say that the desire for God in the heart of a man impels him to make an intellectual assent to God in spite of the weakness of the evidence for such an assent. The will, drawn by love, commands the intellect to believe, but neither is the love in question "affective" nor is the act of the intellect dependent for its existence on the compulsion of the will. If the latter is the cause of faith, it is so only as an efficient cause, not as the formal or the final cause; and it is these latter which pertain to a thing's being. Moreover, if on one hand St. Thomas agrees that charity quickens faith, he argues with equal cogency that faith precedes and in some sense causes charity. "For the movement of the appetite can-not tend to anything, either by hoping or loving, unless that thing be apprehended by the sense or by the intellect. Now it is by faith that the intellect apprehends the object of hope and love" (*ST,* II [1], 62, 4). In other words a man cannot love God until he believes in Him, though he may believe in Him without loving Him. The effect of Newman's emphasis is to reverse that distinction and to suggest that love, considered as strongly affective, makes belief possible; and though he admits the existence of a *fides formata ratione,* "which an infidel may have," his emphasis is elsewhere.

These considerations lead us to the rather surprising con-clusion that Aquinas's conception of faith is more thoroughly supernatural than Newman's. I say "surprising," for we normally think of the Schoolman's confidence in nature and reason as muting the sharp distinction between the natural and the supernatural and of drawing faith and reason closer together, whereas the distrust of reason which Newman shares with so many of his contemporaries is usually regarded (and we have so regarded it here) as making a sharp distinction between nature and grace and of placing a very heavy emphasis on the latter. However, when we examine the matter closely, we discover that the very opposite is the case; that St. Thomas's confidence in the conceptual reason, his reliance on metaphysical as well as on theological wisdom, gives him a freedom from the limitations of nature and reason that Newman never wins.

The explanation of this apparent paradox is to be found in the question of what causes faith, what gives it its being. Newman, though he places the act of faith itself in the intellect, implies that the cause of that act is the compulsion of the heart and will, the whole man's desire for God which precedes assent. Aquinas reserves the form of faith to the intellect itself, and the question which that reservation raises is "what is it that plants that form in the intellect?" If the will, moved by charity, cannot form the intellect to belief, what power can? St. Thomas's answer is, quite simply, God; and in that answer we see why his interpretation of the Catholic doctrine of faith must be regarded as more thoroughly supernatural than Newman's. Of course Newman argues that it is God which stirs in us those "feelings which make us think evidence sufficient, which falls short of a proof in itself"; that "these are feelings not natural to fallen man, and they come only of supernatural grace" (*Sermons,* p. 193). However, such a line of reasoning places a secondary cause as mediary between the action of God and the act of the intellect and subjects faith to the control of our affections and faculties. It is wholly logical for Newman to follow such a course, for he believes the intellect, on account of its conceptual nature, to be less immediately susceptible to assent than the affections; after all, the latter are capable of apprehension and intuition and it is through the latter, primarily, that the conscience speaks. For Aquinas, however, because he trusts the intellect to know truth in concepts—even the divine truth which faith reveals—there is no need for an affective mediation between God and the intellect. Rather he teaches that faith is given being, is formed, in man by the touch of God on the very quick of the intellect.

"Two things," he maintains, "are requisite for faith. First, that the things which are of faith should be proposed to man: this is necessary in order that man believe anything explicitly. The second thing requisite for faith is the assent of the believer to the things which are proposed to him" (*ST*, II [2], 6, 1). On both counts faith must be regarded as being directly from God; for what is proposed to be believed is given in Scripture and tradition by divine revelation, and the assent to those things is caused by the action of God. On the first matter there is no disagreement at all between Aquinas and Newman. The difference with regard to the second we have already indicated. Newman would agree that assent is attributable to the action of God, but he conceives God's eliciting that assent through the medium of the will and affections, through the activities of the implicit reason or the illative sense, through the composite experience of "the whole man."

For Aquinas, for reasons we have already indicated, such an explanation is unsatisfactory or even philosophically impossible; for it overlooks the fact that a habit of the intellect cannot take its being from powers of the soul distinct from the intellect. Moreover, since the intellect is the highest power in the hierarchical order of the soul's faculties, it would be unfitting that God should work through the lower powers to cause belief in the higher. Rather, as we have seen, it is necessary for faith, residing in the intellect, to precede charity, residing in the will; for though absolutely speaking charity is greater than faith, it is nevertheless the habit of a lower faculty and must needs follow and depend upon the habit of the higher. (Nor is charity necessarily greater than the sight or vision which, in heaven, will supersede faith and which is also a habit of the intellect.) Therefore, since faith is not natural to man, since it must be infused in man from without and since that infusion must be directly to the intellect, it follows that faith is formed directly there and that the intellect is moved to assent by the immediate action of God, independently of the other powers of the soul. The Pelagians held that once God proposed to man the matter of belief it was within man's power to assent to those things proposed. "But this," says St. Thomas, "is false, for, since man, by assenting to matters of faith, is raised above his nature, this must needs accrue to him from some supernatural principle moving him inwardly; *and this is God.* Therefore faith, as regards the assent which is the chief act of faith, is *from God moving man inwardly by grace*" (*ST,* II [2], 6, 1; italics added).

From these considerations we see immediately why it is that the Thomist confidence in the intellect gives it its full supernatural liberty in a way that Newman's conception of faith cannot do. Since the intellect is created to be completed or perfected by faith, it follows logically that when God moves that intellect to assent He in no way violates it or constrains it to some activity which is contrary to its proper disposition. Rather, that direct contact between the intellect and God is precisely what the intellect needs to make it whole. It is created to know the universal reality, and that is precisely what the presence of God forming faith in it makes available to it. On the contrary, if we accept Newman's basic emphasis —his presupposition, indeed his haunting fear, that unbelief may be more nearly natural to the conceptual reason than belief—the action of God in inducing assent takes on the quality of a compulsion, of an act by which the intellect, under duress of the lower faculties of the soul, is forced to do something which, though concordant with its nature "in the abstract," is seldom or perhaps never so in fact. Once the notion of compulsion and of the intellect's resistance to faith takes possession of the mind—and since we share with Newman the presuppositions of a scientifically oriented and secular age it is probable that those notions have possession in most of us whether we are aware of them or not—it is logical to argue that the intellect must be moved against its disposition in order to make an assent to God. It is even logical to emphasize the affective aspect of the assent itself, for in such a view desire redeems intellection. Gibbon and his contemporaries did their work too well; they left even orthodox Catholic theologians half persuaded.

However, though we may grant the logic of the conclusion in light of the premises, the validity of the premises, of the secular conception of reason, remains in doubt. We, on account of the revival of Thomist studies since 1879, may now survey the differences with an equal mind. When we do so, when we consider the limitations which intellectual scepticism imposes on Christian thought, when we consider the vast falling off which distinguishes modern Christian poetry from the *Divine Comedy* and which is attributable to the secular limitations of modern theology and the very nearly total absence in our times of Christian metaphysics, we are inclined to argue that the proof of the pudding is in the eating. St. Thomas's confidence in the intellect and in its capacity for metaphysical wisdom and his thorough supernaturalism which is the theological complement of that confidence, give him more to possess and to delight in than Newman dreams of. St. Thomas's possession extends to all that he believes—to all the intellect knows by faith.

III

It remains to speak explicitly of theological wisdom, which, according to St. Thomas, is rooted in faith and grows in the intellect. Because faith is implanted by God directly in the intellect, it is possible for divine things, once they are believed in, to become the principles of knowledge. Indeed to define faith as the substance of things hoped for and to define substance as "the first thing in a genus [which] contains the others virtually," is in effect to say that faith grasps that principle of a thing's being by which knowledge of the thing becomes possible. In other words we might say that faith makes those unseen things of God (impossibly but none the less truly) present in the intellect in a fashion analogous to that in which knowledge unites the form of the thing known to the form of the knowing intellect. Consequently it is possible to define theology as a science, and St. Thomas defends that definition on the grounds that though theology takes its subject matter from things believed rather than, as metaphysics does, from things naturally known, the things believed serve as legitimate principles of intellectual activity.

He begins the *Summa Theologica* with the question of "whether sacred doctrine is a science," and he answers affirmatively (I, 1, 2). Moreover the principal objections to which he directs his answers are fairly close to Newman's propositions concerning notions and images—so close, in fact, that we might even say that Aquinas anticipates Newman's anti-intellectualism. The first of those objections is that since all knowledge which man acquires by natural reason proceeds "from self-evident principles" whereas "sacred doctrine proceeds from articles of faith which are not self-evident," sacred doctrine cannot be regarded as a legitimate science (I, 1, 2). The force of the objection is clearly one that Newman felt very strongly, and, as we have seen, it impels him to transfer the motive power of faith from the intellect to the affections and the will and to maintain that faith exercises itself upon weaker evidence than that on which the sciences work.

In effect Newman admits the truth of the objection and proceeds to "save" the truth of faith by denying, so far as his orthodoxy allows him, that theology is truly scientific. Some propositions which constitute the Catholic faith are, he admits, undeniably notional propositions; in fact even so high a doctrine as the mystery of the Holy Trinity requires a notional or scientific assent. Therefore it is necessary to grant that the edifice of sacred doctrine depends at some very important points on notions. However, such notions as the doctrine of the Trinity are susceptible to a type of real assent, and that in two ways. First, though the doctrine of the Trinity *qua* doctrine can only be apprehended as a notion or concept, its various constituent aspects—the Persons of Father, Son, and Holy Ghost—can be received affectively or intuitively, in such a fashion that they may take a "personal hold" upon the believer. Second, these unavoidably notional propositions are guaranteed by the infallible authority of the Church, and that authority, exercised as it is by men in an historical context, can be a legitimate object of real apprehension and thus of real assent. Therefore, though aspects of Christian theology may be notional, the impact even of those aspects is not purely conceptual or scientific. Meanwhile the great body of *de fide* propositions in Christian theology are brought before believers not as notions but as images, and principal among those images is that of Christ Himself who, as man, is susceptible to other men's direct or personal apprehension. Thus Newman speaks of Christ's, "through His preachers," having "imprinted the Image or Idea of Himself in the minds of His subjects individually"; and he insists that it is a real assent to that image rather than a notional assent to "a corporate body or a doctrine" which has inspired the zeal of saints and martyrs (*Grammar,* pp. 353–54).

Thus we may say that Newman admits the objection that theology is "unscientific"—not, at its most characteristic, the subject of concepts. St. Thomas meets the objection with the argument that "there are two kinds of sciences," one of which proceeds from a principle "known by the natural light of the intelligence" and another which depends upon principles "known by the light of a higher science." Examples of the former are arithmetic and geometry; of the latter, perspective, which proceeds from the principles established by geometry. Sacred doctrine is a science of the latter sort "because it proceeds from principles established by the light of a higher science, namely, the science of God and the blessed" (*ST,* I, I, 2). When we recall that by science Aquinas does in fact mean knowledge in the sense that we have defined it—as the literal union of the form of the thing known with the intellect of the knower and the utterance of that union in a notion—

we see how exact this definition of sacred science is. He is saying in effect that the subject matter of faith, namely God and the blessed, can enter as intelligible species into the intellect of the believer to fecundate that intellect. That subject matter differs from the subject matter of merely natural or human science, including metaphysics, in that it is revealed by God and believed in by faith rather than demonstrated by reason, but insofar as it is a subject of intellection it has the same relationship to the believer as merely human knowledge has to him who knows and proves it. In short, sacred doctrine, the articles of faith in their full notional development, constitute a genuine science.

Aquinas's second objection, which also anticipates Newman's teaching, is that sacred doctrine is not a science because it deals with "individual facts, such as the deeds of Abraham, Isaac, and Jacob," whereas a science, by definition, deals with notions or concepts, not facts. It is interesting that in this instance what St. Thomas sees as an objection to the scientific validity of theology, Newman, distrusting concepts, sees as one of theology's strengths. Indeed he seeks the "reality" of religion in just such "individual facts"—he would call them images—as Abraham, Isaac, Jacob, and all the other personages and histories which Scripture records. What Newman does not seem to realize is that individual facts, individual people, cannot be *known*. Aquinas, well aware of the distinction between sense impressions or images (phantasms) on one hand and true knowledge in concept on the other, sees immediately that if the subject matter of faith is to be something that man can know with the same (or greater) certitude that he can know arithmetic or geometry, it cannot be simply a congeries of images or concrete singular things. Therefore he answers the objection in a manner that cuts withershins across Newman's whole conception of belief. "Individual facts," he says, "are treated of in sacred doctrine, not because it is concerned with them principally"; they are introduced in Scripture "as examples to be followed in our lives" and "in order to establish the authority of those men through whom the divine revelation . . . has come down to us" (*ST*, I, I, 2). However, that revelation itself is not a group of individual facts but rather the *quiddities* of those facts—the forms which make them what they are; for it is the forms, as intelligible species, which are assimilable to the human intellect and which make a science of divine things possible.

Once we grasp these principles fully, we are in a position to understand how St. Thomas (and Dante) can speak with assurance of a genuine knowledge, still conceptual, not mystical, of even such mysterious and holy realities as the Godhead itself. Man cannot know God's essence, but he can make use of His "effects, either of nature or of grace, in place of a definition," and thereby come to a true, if incomplete, knowledge of Him; "even as in some philosophical sciences we demonstrate something about a cause from its effect, by taking the effect in place of a definition of the cause" (*ST*, I, I, 7). Moreover, because the knowledge of God by faith is in fact subject to the same rules that apply to the knowledge of lower things, to other sciences, sacred doctrine can be treated as "a matter of argument." That does not mean that the principles of sacred doctrine, the articles of faith, are subject to debate, for no science argues in proof of its principles. Rather every science argues from its principles, from those understood truths on which it is predicated, to demonstrate other dependent truths. Sacred science is no exception to that rule. Arguing from articles of faith, it proceeds to other truths, and in doing so it makes proper use of human reason. For since "grace does not destroy nature, but perfects it," it follows that "natural reason should minister to faith" (*ST*, I, I, 8). However, it takes only a moment's reflection to see that the latter would be an impossible ministry unless the subject matter of faith were assimilable as concepts to the intellect; for the reason can only deal with things known, not with things apprehended or assented to in images by the senses and imagination.

From these considerations follows a third principle of Thomist teaching on the nature of theological wisdom—that not only the articles of faith per se but their elaboration can be rested on as true. As Gilson interprets these portions of the *Summa,* "revelation resides in us only to the extent that we can be said to know it," and within the Church there is a hierarchy of such knowledge, ranging from "the Christian Doctor to the simple faithful." That means that the legitimate elaborations of the creeds and the Scriptures in works such as the *Summa* have a validity analogous to that of the creeds themselves. In fact the science of theology even in its most extensive (Newman would say its most fully notional) development has the same *reality* as Holy Scripture from which it springs. In fact, as Gilson says, it "is nothing else than Holy Scripture received into the human understanding, or, to put it in another way, it is only divine revelation spreading itself, thanks to the light of a reason which examines the content of faith, the authority of faith and the ends of faith." [5] Thus in Thomist theory the wall of division between revealed knowledge and acquired knowledge, between things known by faith and things known by reason, is broken down, leaving the way open for the theologian (or the poet who depends upon a theologian) to proceed from the articles of faith to a full, rational understanding of the whole order of being. Aquinas argues, for instance, that by faith man comes not only to an understanding of the "First Truth" but also of "many other things" in their relationship to the "First Truth" (*ST,* II [2], I, I). Therefore when Dante relates the forms of all things—earth, air, fire and water—as well as the structure of the universe to the life of the Holy Trinity, or when he depicts the universal form of all creation in the Second Person or Word of the Father, he might be said to be exploiting the resources of theology—resources which it possesses by virtue of its being a legitimate science. A theology built on real apprehensions or intuitions (if indeed we can call it a theology) has no such resources; its subject matter is not susceptible to conceptual elaboration. The loss of the validity of the concept not only shatters metaphysics but limits radically the scope of theology's possession.

Hopkins, Newman, and Scotus

Gerard Manley Hopkins as metaphysician, theologian, and poet suffered from that limitation of scope, from that curtailment of possession and keen delight, which is the consequence of modern scepticism's impinging on Catholic thought.

In part at least that limitation is a consequence of Newman's influence, but in how large a part it is difficult to say. There is no problem about documenting the relationship between the two men with reference to their correspondence, their personal acquaintance and Hopkins's familiarity with Newman's work;[1] and one can surmise that Hopkins was both familiar and at least in some measure sympathetic with Newman's philosophical position. On the other hand it is perfectly possible to argue that there is nothing in Hopkins's thought which might not have been derived from other sources. Hopkins, like Newman, stresses intuitive at the expense of conceptual cognition, and consequently, like Newman, he places a great deal of emphasis on the existing individual as the senses apprehend him rather than on the notion of that individual which the intellect abstracts; but so too does almost every major literary figure in Victorian England, including Pater, whose influence on Hopkins is indisputable. Indeed that emphasis is an inheritance from Wordsworth, Coleridge, and the other Romantics which in one way or another shapes the thought of all major writers of the age. Therefore when Hopkins speaks of instressing an inscape, though it is tempting to explain *instress* with reference to "real apprehension," we must remember that Hopkins never uses Newman's phrase in his own aesthetic or theological writings and that, stripped of its specifically Christian connotations, *instress* is virtually indistinguishable from Words-worth's intuitive seeing "into the life of things."[2]

On the other hand, even granting these reservations, it would be a mistake to discount Newman's influence altogether; for the very fact that *instress* does have Christian connotations is a matter we cannot afford to ignore and a matter which is more difficult to account for without a consideration of New-man's influence than with it. The reason is that Newman anticipates Hopkins in one respect in which Wordsworth, Coleridge, and Pater clearly do not: Newman unites the popu-lar scepticism and subjectivism of the age with a rigorous adherence to Catholic dogma. Though we may take that union for granted now, we must not forget that when Newman's thought was insinuating itself into the nineteenth-century Catholic revival, that union was revolutionary. Seldom before —and never on so broad a scale—had orthodox Catholicism been consciously, even deliberately, antimetaphysical in its bias. Though we may grant the presence of a sceptical strain in patristic and Augustinian Platonism—a strain which St. Thomas identifies and repudiates—it is safe to say that except in a few instances, such as that of Tertullian,[3] the older the-ology, like Scholasticism though in a different way and degree, embraced metaphysical wisdom as its adjunct. Certainly from the time of the Scholastic flowering in the thirteenth century until the Catholic revival in the nineteenth that theology had not only been permeated with metaphysics but rigorously in-tellectual and systematic in its formulation. That it is so now in a less profound degree is due in considerable measure to the fact that Newman's work was both revolutionary in reference to the past and influential (for better or worse) in reference to the future;[4] and Hopkins appears to have been one of the earliest recipients of that influence. We might say that Hopkins yoked together (possibly by violence) the doctrine of Dante and the sensibility of Wordsworth—a yoking that probably could not have been effected without Newman's example. For even though Hopkins may not have followed that example consciously, the very fact that Newman, whose path to Rome Hopkins *did* follow, had been able to accept Catholicism in its full dogmatic development without relinquishing contemporary modes of secular thought would have, so to speak, cleared the way for Hopkins to do the same. Indeed, on account of Newman's example it is possible that Hopkins may have entered the Church of Rome in relative innocence of the fact that hitherto (and even then in many quarters, as in some quarters now) intellectual scepticism was considered irreconcilable with dogmatic orthodoxy. After all, it was not until he became a Jesuit that Hopkins became acquainted with the Scholastics.

Moreover when he did make their acquaintance it was Scotus whom he preferred to St. Thomas, and that preference might well be regarded as a logical consequence of Newman's influence. That is certainly not to say that Scotus is himself a philosophical sceptic, but it is easier to interpret his thought in that fashion than it is St. Thomas's. For instance it is easy to see why a young man who had read the *Apologia,* the *Difficulties of Anglicans,* and the *Discourses on University Education* during the period of his life when his religious opinions were being shaped would have been drawn to Scotus's high doctrine of individuality and to his theory of intuitive cognition. Indeed the former corresponds very closely to Newman's persistent emphasis on the uniqueness of every creature as it is brought "before us" by the senses rather than as generalized by a notion, and the latter to his preference of the "whole man's" real apprehension to the intellect's conceptual understanding.

There is even some indication that Hopkins may have made a conscious association of Newman and Scotus. We know, for instance, that he read the *Grammar of Assent* for the first time almost exactly a year after (and in the same place) he made his famous discovery of the *Opus Oxoniense.* That was in 1872 and 1873, on the Isle of Man.[5] We know that during the next decade, which was precisely the period of Scotus's greatest influence upon him, Hopkins also kept up sufficient interest in Newman that in 1883 he asked the latter's permission to write a "comment" on the *Grammar*.[6] What that "comment," had Newman granted permission, might have said we can only guess; but certainly Christopher Devlin's suggestion that it would have been an interpretation of Newman's major theses "in the light of [Hopkins's] own Scotist scholastic principles" seems plausible.[7] In short the external evidence leads us to suppose that during the decade from 1873 to 1883, the decade in which Hopkins wrote all his major poetry save for the "terrible sonnets," he was occupied theologically and philosophically with both Newman and Scotus. So far from the similarities between the two having escaped him, he was sufficiently struck by those similarities that at the end of that decade he was prepared to apply the more nearly systematic thought of the one to an interpretation of the other. Let us consider, therefore, Hopkins's debt to Scotus as well as his modifications of Scotist ideas, remaining cognizant as we do so of the similarities between Scotus and Newman.

II

The aspect of Scotus's thought in which he most nearly resembles Newman and also that in which Hopkins was evidently most interested is his epistemology.[8] Our point of departure for understanding that epistemology is a recognition of the fact that Scotus is Augustinian and therefore indirectly Platonist (as we have seen Newman, in some measure, to be) rather than Thomist and Aristotelian in his basic philosophical assumptions. He attempted a synthesis between Thomist and Augustinian teaching, and he found himself to be in agreement with many of St. Thomas's fundamental propositions; but as Efrem Bettoni makes clear, his intention was "to assimilate Thomistic Aristotelianism" to Augustinianism rather than the other way around. Hence, as Bettoni demonstrates, even when he criticizes Henry of Ghent's Augustinian positions, Scotus's aim is to purify rather than to contradict those positions; for, like Henry and unlike Aquinas, "he himself moves within the

. . . Platonic-Augustinian line of thought, from which he does not depart unless forced to do so."[9] As we have seen, the primary epistemological distinction between the Augustinian and the Thomist schools is that whereas the latter relies for knowledge upon intelligible species abstracted from existing substances, the former appeals in one fashion or another (depending on the particular Augustinian theologian in question) to the intellect's direct participation of the forms.

Scotus's synthesis involves taking what he no doubt conceived to be the best of those two epistemological worlds. On one hand he agrees with St. Thomas that the human mind acquires intelligible species by abstraction from sense experience. However, abstraction as Scotus understands it is radically different from what Aquinas conceives the process to be; for in Scotus's thought the role of the intellect is much more nearly Augustinian than Thomist. For instance, he rejects the fundamental Thomist doctrine that the phantasm is the cause of intellection, that the mind is moved to know by what the senses perceive. Such a doctrine, in his estimation, infringes upon the prerogatives of the intellect, reducing its role to that of a mere mirror of external things. Therefore he places his emphasis, in typically Augustinian fashion, not on the thing as it impregnates the intellect by means of an intelligible species, but upon a mode of union between intellect and thing in which the soul gives as much as it receives.

That mode of union is best described as one in which the intelligible species, rather than being abstracted from the phantasm by the agent intellect, is engendered by the agent in the possible intellect in response to the presence of the phantasm. As Gilson explains the process, the sensible species or phantasm is only a partial cause of knowledge: *l'autre cause partielle est l'intellect agent, dont le rôle est précisément d'engendrer une espèce de même nature que lui, c'est-à-dire intelligible et capable d'universalité.*[10] It takes only a moment's reflection to see that the species thus engendered must be regarded, not as the intention or promotion of the thing in the intellect (which Scotus calls the *intentio realis*),[11] but rather as the intellect's utterance of itself in response to the stimulation of the thing. Therefore Scotus concludes that though the phantasm (the sensible or singular species) is necessary for cognition as a catalyst to knowledge, knowledge itself springs from the intellect and from the intellect alone.

The consequence of such a theory of knowledge is that whereas for St. Thomas the intelligible species which seeds the intellect, because it is abstracted from the phantasm of the thing, effects a real union between the knower and the thing known, for Scotus that engendering species, though impossible of conception without the presence of the phantasm, is ultimately other than the thing. Thus we are forced to conclude that though Scotus holds to a doctrine of abstraction *a sensu,* of acquired species, his interpretation of that doctrine is such as to distinguish him radically from St. Thomas. Scotus does not deny the objectivity, the *reality,* of conceptual knowledge; he does not go so far as Newman does, to say that notions, or the sciences built on notions, are no more than subjective reflections of objective truth or that notions starve and dilute reality. However, one can see how such sceptical views might be said to be latent in his theory of abstraction and why Hopkins, already informed by those sceptical opinions, might be drawn to Scotus by them.

On the other hand it was probably not to the latent scepticism as such—to the distrust of abstraction in itself—that Hopkins was attracted but rather to its corollary: Scotus's doctrine of intuitive cognition which so closely resembles Hopkins's instress. Scotus defines intuition as a mode of intellection, not of sensation; it would be unfair of us to ignore that fact. We have already distinguished between the Scholastic and modern uses of intuition, and we must recall at this point that for the former intuition is genuinely cognitive.[12] It signifies direct intellection rather than indirect, but directness does not involve, as it does for many modern thinkers, the extinction of intellect. On the other hand, just as Scotus's theory of abstraction moves toward, without reaching, the pole of notional scepticism, so, too, his theory of intuition anticipates, without becoming, the modern substitution of sensation and imagination for understanding—of real apprehension for notional. Indeed, as we shall see, it is that tendency in his theory which makes intuition susceptible to Hopkins's appropriation as instress; and the key to that tendency is Scotus's definition of intuition as a mode of cognition which knows a thing *secundum quod existens, et secundum quod praesens in aliqua existentia actuali* (according as it is existing, and according as it is present in some actually existing thing).[13] He calls it elsewhere a *visio . . . exsistentis ut exsistens est et ut praesens est videnti secundum suam exsistentiam* (a perception of an existence seen as it is existing and as it is present according to its existence).[14] In other words intuitive cognition is of the individually existing thing, the thing in itself, in its actuality. Abstractive cognition, on the contrary, is not of the thing but rather of the thing's quiddity or nature, *secundum quod abstrahitur ab existentia actuali, et non existentia* (according as it has been abstracted from actual existence, and not existing).[15] In short, intuitive cognition grasps the existent reality of the thing known whereas abstractive cognition concerns itself with the thing's essence, abstracted from the thing itself.

One sees immediately that however diverse in some respects their epistemologies may be, Scotus and Newman both contradict the same Thomist principles. Though Scotus does not go so far as Newman in questioning the validity of abstractive cognition and though he insists that intuition is genuinely cognitive, his distinction between the two modes of intellection resembles Newman's distinction between notional and real apprehension in that it tends to isolate the thing from the concept of its quiddity and to assign a separate mode of cognition to each. For Aquinas on the other hand, because the form of a thing is literally *of* the thing and not to be understood as having existence apart from the existence of the composite, the distinction between the two modes of cognition is eliminated. To know the quiddity of a thing is, by definition, to know the thing, nor can we even speak of knowing the thing in itself, as existing, except reflexively, after the abstraction and conception of its quiddity. Therefore, whereas Scotus relies upon intuition for knowledge of the individual substance, Aquinas relies on *compositio* or judgment—the "third act of knowledge"—which can be regarded as the epistemological corollary of his doctrine of the nature of individual existence. Since the intention of the form as intelligible species is the *quo est* rather than the *quod est* in respect of knowledge, it is necessary, once the abstraction and the formation of the concept have taken place, to reunite the notion with the thing. Indeed by doing so the intellect demonstrates its fidelity to the real, ratifying by an act of composition the composite nature of the substance which it knows. In other words we might say that in the third act of intellection the mind imitates the structure of the substance (*ST,* I, 85, 5). It is for that reason, as Gilson says, that *compositio* "can penetrate to existence"[16]—a penetration which, for Scotus, is accomplished in the first act of knowledge, by intuition. The manifest advantage of St. Thomas's doctrine over Scotus's is that it preserves the unity of quiddity and substance and prevents a separation of the thing-in-itself from a knowledge of its quiddity.

Scotus not only allows for such a separation; he encourages it with his teaching that abstractive cognition is not natural or proper to the human intellect but is, rather, a consequence of the fall. Abstraction *is* necessary for human intellection but only, in Scotus's favorite phrase, *pro statu isto,* in the circumstances of this present life in a fallen world. Had it not been for the fall, he says, men would have been as angels with respect to cognition—they would have known intuitively not only substances but the essences or quiddities of those substances for which, as things now stand, we must rely upon abstraction. Though an absolute necessity, abstraction must be regarded as a makeshift, a necessary evil, a means of filling a gap left by man's original defection from a pristine state in which all knowledge would have been as sight, as *visio.* Beyond the veil, in reference to the beatific vision, we shall see face to face; and, had we not been disobedient children, we should be seeing face to face here and now. However, even in our fallen condition we have preserved the capacity for intuition of existing singular substances, and that intuition is preliminary and indispensable to the supplementary process of abstraction by which we for the moment make do.

III

When we turn from questions of epistemology per se to their metaphysical ramifications, it is that supplementary process of abstraction with which we must deal initially. That is so because the proper object of metaphysics and consequently the basis for a natural knowledge of God is what Scotus calls being *qua* being without reference to distinctions between individuals and species or between things sensible and things spiritual. That common being, of which God may be described as an infinite degree or mode and upon which, consequently, a proof of His existence rests, can only be known fully and accurately by abstraction—in concept. That such is the case should not surprise us when we consider the matter carefully; for if man, *pro statu isto,* is deprived of the *visio* of the essences of composite substances, we should scarcely expect him to retain that capacity in reference to the universal essence and certainly not in reference to its infinite degree. Indeed we may say that on account of the fall metaphysical wisdom is constrained to be abstract.

Since intuition rather than abstraction is proper to man, we are not surprised that Scotus allows for at least one relaxation of that general constraint—an allowance of which Hopkins might be said to have taken advantage in his appropriation and adaptation of Scotus. I refer to Scotus's teaching that a knowledge of common being is implicit, present inchoately and confusedly, in our original intuition of an individually existing substance. As Gilson explains the matter, *Il est certain que l'intellect ne commence pas par saisir distinctement le concept commun d'être pris dans son indétermination totale.* Rather knowledge of common being begins *par des concepts confus, dont chacun représente l'un des objets d'expérience auxquels nous donnons des noms*—names, not definitions or concepts.[17] Gilson's use here of the participle *confused* is very much to the point. Scotus uses *confused cognition* interchangeably with *intuition* and *distinct cognition* interchangeably with *abstraction.* Both terms in each pair signify the same mode of intellection, but their connotations differ; and in the present context, where we refer to an implicit and inchoate knowledge of common being in the singular substance, it makes sense to speak of intuition as confused cognition. The following statement by Father Christopher Devlin seems to make Scotus's point with even greater precision than Gilson does: "Every distinct act of knowing . . . has been preceded by a first act wherein sense and intellect are one, a confused intuition of Nature as a living whole [we may read, 'of common being'], though the effect of the senses is to contract this intuition to a particular 'glimpse,' which is called the 'species specialissima.' "[18] In other words, in every intuition of a singular existence *sicut est in se* we do know confusedly and in contracted form that being which is common to all things and by which we know God.

Scotus explains the contraction by reference to the power of sensation which is involved in the intuition of singular existing things. On account of that involvement we know first, confusedly, that being which moves our senses more powerfully: *Quodcumque enim individuum fortius movet sensum, eius species prius cognita est cognitione confusa* (indeed whatever individual being moves the sense more strongly, its species is known first in a confused cognition).[19] Consequently, *quoad primum illum actum non est in potestate nostra quid intelligamus* (as far as that first act is concerned, what we know is not in our power);[20] for though any species may be capable of moving the mind to intellection, it may be impeded in doing so by another species which moves it more forcibly. Singular beings move the sense more forcibly than do the distinct concepts of essences and certainly more forcibly than does the concept of being *qua* being in complete indetermination. Therefore we grasp that common being first in the singular—in the *species specialissima.* That apprehension, as Gilson explains, is necessarily confused because *nous ne connaissons pas le singulier*—"*pro statu isto*"—*sous sa raison propre de singulier.*[21] By its very singularity it is unsusceptible of concept, of definition.

Therefore once that confused, intuitive grasp of common being contracted to the singular takes place, the intellect immediately passes beyond it to distinct cognition, from *visio* to conceptual understanding. Indeed there seems no question but that Scotus understands confused cognition of common being as no more, *pro statu isto,* than a first step to distinct; and we might describe Hopkins's modification of Scotist teaching by saying that he chooses not to take the second step. Rather he attempts to achieve knowledge of God by exclusive reliance upon confused cognition of singulars, and by doing so he might be said to exploit the dissociation of sensibility latent in Scotist teaching. The greater integrity of Thomism allows no opportunity for such exploitation.

IV

With regard to this fundamental difference between Hopkins and Scotus, Christopher Devlin is less helpful than he is in other facets of his studies.[22] The reason for that deficiency is that he, so to speak, reads Hopkins back into Scotus and thus sees Scotus through Hopkins's eyes. He says, for instance, in reference to Scotus, not Hopkins, that "in the process of abstraction, the vague (*indeterminata*) but alive nature becomes petrified into a number of distinct notions concerning its various properties and qualities. Without vision [*visio*], these soon become remote from the living reality that fathered them."[23] In strictest denotative terms Father Devlin's analysis is correct. As we have seen, Scotus does prefer intuition and considers it natural to man. However, it is clear that the connotation he bestows upon that analysis is not truly Scotist. The association of petrification with abstraction is finally foreign to Scotus's mode of thought, for though abstraction is only a necessity *pro statu isto,* a necessity it certainly is; and

Scotus is not likely to define the concept of being *qua* being, which is the *proper* object of human intellection, the *raison d'être* of metaphysics, and the fundamental ground of a natural knowledge of God—though only for the time being—with *petrification*.

That Hopkins might well use such a noun in such a context, that by stopping short with confused cognition he in effect evades the whole order of conceptual knowledge, probably owes as much to Wordsworth, Pater, and Newman as to Scotus. To rest a knowledge of being and of God on confused cognition of singulars is in effect to transform Scotus's intuition into Kant's—or into real apprehension; and one wonders whether Father Devlin is not too modern, too much persuaded by modern scepticism, to recognize that fact. One doubts that Hopkins himself recognized the difference between his position and Scotus's. The fact that he identifies Scotus with his own concepts of inscape and instress—and without stated qualification—suggests that his age's anti-intellectualism and, in particular, his reading of the *Grammar of Assent* may have insinuated itself into his reading of the *Opus Oxoniense* to such an extent that it led to a confusion of philosophies which, though similar, are in fact distinct. It is Newman (or Pater or the Romantic poets), not Scotus, who says that distinct concepts, when separated from vision, become petrified, "remote from the living reality that fathered them." It is Newman, not Scotus, who allows *visio* to stand alone, in at least a virtual, if not total,[24] independence of abstractive cognition. Therefore when Father Devlin says that the first act of intellection can be isolated from the second and "dwelt on (by 'instress'?) to the exclusion of succeeding abstractions,"[25] he is offering a legitimate interpretation of Hopkins and through Hopkins of Newman, but not of Scotus; for though Scotus allows the possibility of such an isolation, he clearly regards it as contrary to the normal process of cognition for man in this life.

One consequence of such an isolation is the loss of traditional metaphysical poetry; for when one contracts the experience of the reality of being to a pinpoint—to a confused cognition of a *species specialissima*—he thereby deprives the poet of that liberty of heaven and earth which the distinct concept provides. Whether Scotus's metaphysics, even when properly interpreted, can provide that liberty is not here in question. We have seen that both his separation of intuition and abstraction and his doctrine concerning the origin of intelligible species tend to isolate the concept of the thing from the thing itself in its substantial, existential reality. Nevertheless Scotus properly interpreted comes a great deal closer to that liberty than does Newman or than does Scotus interpreted by Hopkins (probably under Newman's influence) or Scotus interpreted by Father Devlin (certainly under Hopkins's influence). The latter reads Hopkins correctly when he says that by dwelling on the "first act . . . to the exclusion of succeeding abstractions, . . . you can feel, see, hear or somehow experience the Nature which is yours and all creation's as 'pattern, air, melody,—what I call *inscape*.' And if you can hold that, then you have a poem 'in petto.' " However, we must remember that Scotus would have insisted that the cognitive process is not complete until that intuitive experience of a common Nature has been translated by abstraction into a distinct concept of being *qua* being and that, regrettably but no less truly, such translation can only take place, *pro statu isto*, when the *visio* is *not* dwelt upon by instress "to the exclusion of succeeding abstractions." Of course Father Devlin adds that one must return to that poem " 'in petto' . . . with the abstractive intelligence" in order to express it,[26] but he does not explain the nature of that return and expression. One gets the impression that his allusion to it is little more than a nominal concession to a side of Scotus's thought which neither he nor Hopkins finds very interesting. Moreover it is worth noting that that is exactly the sort of nominal concession to abstractive cognition which Newman makes—as though to guard his flank or rear against the censure of Scholastic theologians. In any event it requires very little reflection to see that this poem "in petto," considered as the fruit of vision in isolation from abstraction, is the archetypical Hopkinsian poem: the expression of the intuitive and confused cognition of the instress of creation and of God Himself, that stress's source, in the dappled world—in the variety of singular species to which that general, common instress is contracted. Whatever role the abstractive process may play in the utterance of this particular kind of metaphysical wisdom, this intimate intuition of God in the *species specialissima,* the final result will be radically different from a metaphysics and a poetry of Dante's sort in which the metaphors of God are based on the abstraction of quiddities of existing substances.

V

Hopkins's theology, considered as distinct from his intuitive apprehension of God as being in things, amounts to little more than ascribing names and descriptions to that being. When one grasps in a confused cognition the instress of creation, which in its infinite degree is also God, what, in fact, does one grasp? Theology comes to answer the question but, as we should expect, in symbols or even myths rather than in concepts.

Hopkins's theology, like his metaphysics, is built on Scotist propositions—in particular on the suggestion that the Incarnation was not caused by Adam's sin but that the hypostatic union was ordained before the foundation of the world: that in fact the world was created to be united to the Second Person of the Holy Trinity in the Incarnation.

> *Dico tamen quod lapsus non fuit causa predestinationis Christi, imo si nec fuisset Adam lapsus, nec homo, adhuc fuisset Christus sic predestinatus, imo, etsi non fuissent creandi alii quam solus Christus.*[27]
>
> (I say nevertheless that the fall was not the cause of the predestination of Christ; on the contrary if neither Adam nor man had fallen, Christ would still have been predestinated in this manner even though there had been no other created beings save Christ alone.)

From this proposition Hopkins proceeds to elaborate a theological explanation of the source of being, which, stated in its simplest terms, is that the common being or instress of creation is Christ in sacrifice to the Father—what Hopkins calls "the great sacrifice" (see *SD*, pp. 196–202).

It is unnecessary to rehearse the details of Hopkins's doctrine, for they are by now familiar to his readers. Let us simply point to the fundamental proposition on which they rest: that the "inmanning" of the Word took place first, not in Bethlehem, but before the foundation of the world. Prior to His "infleshing"[28] in the temporal order, Christ, already "inmanned," dwelled with the Holy Angels in what Hopkins calls the aeonian order in which the "great sacrifice," the archetype of Calvary and of the Eucharist, took place. That sacrifice is the source of created being, of being or stress outside of God. Hopkins speaks for instance of two "processions" of the Word prior to His "procession" in the flesh in Galilee. The first is the eternal, intrinsic procession of the Son from the Father in the Holy Trinity; the second, which is the first of the two extrinsic processions and which is "less than eternal," is that which takes place in aeonian time. Hopkins calls this first extrinsic procession the "first intention . . . of God outside himself or, as they say, *ad extra,* outwards, the first outstress of God's power." The reason for this outstress was "to give God glory and that by sacrifice, sacrifice offered in the barren wilderness outside of God" (*SD*, p. 197). Therefore Hopkins can speak of that sacrifice as the origin of created being and he can, in light of the theory, maintain that the call to sacrifice, as in martyrdom or as in the celebration of the Eucharist, is a "call into being." Consequently Hopkins considers Christ as "redeemer," not only of man from sin but also "of his own created being [hence of all being, since all creatures were *creati in Christo Jesu*], which he retrieves from nothingness" (*SD*, p. 170).

From a consideration of these doctrines we see why it is reasonable for Hopkins to identify the common being or instress of the whole creation, which he grasps intuitively in the various *species specialissimae,* with Christ in His archetypal sacrifice to the Father. "It is as if the blissful agony or stress of selving in God had forced out drops of sweat or blood, which drops were the world, or as if the lights lit at the festival of the 'peaceful Trinity' through some little cranny striking out lit up into being one 'cleave' out of the world of possible creatures" (*SD,* p. 197). Hopkins's prose expresses the mystery of being as divine sacrifice—or, more accurately, of being as Christ-in-sacrifice—by its very condensation. The "outstress" from God, the issuance of His being into the nothingness outside of Him, is represented here as drops of blood or sweat, and of course we associate the latter with Christ's passion and death. It follows that to participate in being is, by definition, to participate in that archetypal procession and sacrifice in which being is redeemed from nothingness. Therefore we may say that when Hopkins isolates the confused cognition of a thing from subsequent abstraction (when, in his own terms, he instresses an inscape) the common being which reveals itself inchoately in the singular, existing substance is, in some profoundly true sense, Christ's blood.

In most of the poems from 1876 to 1883 (the years in which Hopkins seems to have been under the combined influence of Scotus and Newman) the persona or speaker makes the discovery that Christ-as-sacrifice is the being of things. The moment of high drama in most of these poems is that in which the intuition of being takes place; and the drama is intensified by the fact that, given theology's description of being, the intuition invariably demands sacrifice on the part of the beholder. Since being is Christ-as-sacrifice, to know it immediately and by intuition rather than in notion one must participate in some measure in that sacrifice. One thinks of the tall nun's "martyrdom" and of the way in which Hopkins associates her with the stigmata of St. Francis. She is, literally speaking, neither a martyr nor a stigmatic, but both associations suggest that her apprehension of Christ as "Ground of being, and granite of it" demands participation in His blood.[29]

A typical instance of the persona as beholder or discoverer

of Christ's stress in the being of things is to be found in "The Starlight Night." The octave presents the rich variegation of the world: the stars themselves, the things which glow in the woods at night, the frost on cold lawns, and the whitebeam. These various *species specialissimae* are offered to us as objects whose beauty is so great as to induce rapture or ecstasy in the beholder—"Look at the stars! look, look up at the skies!" However, the question implicit in the octave of the sonnet is how the beholder is to apprehend them or enter into an immediate experience of their beauty: what must one pay or bid in order to buy or win this beauty? Hopkins answers, "Prayer, patience, alms, vows." It seems a curious response, a *non sequitur,* for what connection, we wonder, can there be between the sight of the splendor of the night sky and this encouragement to a devout and holy life. The answer, of course, lies in Hopkins's identification of the being of these dazzling, dappled things with the very flesh and blood of Christ. Once we acknowledge that identification and once we recognize that prayer, patience, alms, and vows, being modes of sacrifice, are means of participating in "the great sacrifice" and, therefore, in Christ's flesh and blood, we see how appropriate, in fact, the answer is. By living a sacrificial life we share in Christ's sacrifice which is the "call into being." Consequently by that same sacrificial life we share, as it were, in the being of all creatures. Once we make that discovery, the rich variegated beauty of heaven and earth yields its meaning:

> These are indeed the barn; withindoors house
> The shocks. This piece-bright paling shuts the spouse
>   Christ home, Christ and his mother and all his
>   hallows.

The harvest imagery is interesting, for just prior to these lines Hopkins has described the rich configuration of individual existences in two summary metaphors: "May-mess" and "March-bloom." What blooms in March and May yields fruit for harvest later, and the implication of the imagery seems to be that the beholder, by heeding the call to sacrifice and thus to being, has enabled himself to harvest Christ from the *species specialissimae* which constitute the world—"Down all that glory in the heavens to glean our Saviour" ("Hurrahing in Harvest").

VI

A similar gleaning takes place in most of the poems between "The Wreck of the Deutschland" and the beginning of the terrible sonnets, but I cite "The Starlight Night" rather than "The Windhover" or "God's Grandeur" or "Pied Beauty" because it manifests with especial clarity not only Hopkins's characteristic mode of apprehension but also the central difficulty inherent in it: how to bestow unity upon a vision of the world which is made up of distinct intuitions of individual existences. In the case of "The Starlight Night" the question takes the form of whether the details which begin with "diamond delves" in line four are supposed to be metaphors for the stars or whether each is important in its own right. Has Hopkins, at that point in the poem, turned his gaze from heaven to earth and simply added details to the scene he is describing, or has he called upon his recollection of things which glow in the woods at night, of leaves in the wind, of doves in a farmyard, to illustrate what he sees in the sky? Such distinguished Hopkinsians as J. Hillis Miller, John Pick, and W. H. Gardner read the poem on the latter assumption, but I rather agree with Elisabeth Schneider that the former is more likely the correct one.[30] She makes the astute observation that extended and fanciful metaphor is not characteristic of Hopkins, and she therefore prefers to read the diamond delves and all the details that follow as distinct constituents, along with the stars, of the "scape" which Hopkins is describing. On the other hand she is frank to admit that the latter reading also raises questions, and the most obvious, I believe, is what relation these various details have to one another. If they are not a series of metaphors for the stars, what do these bright fragments have in common?

The textbook answer is that they have Christ in common, and it is clear from Hopkins's imagery that that is the answer he would have us give. The stars, as "fire-folk," are compared to the saints in heaven, and saints are the members of Christ's body, epiphanies of His incarnation and, hence, of the "great sacrifice." The implication is that to behold the stars, as to behold the heavenly radiance of the "hallows," is to behold Christ Himself. The ontological (or Christological) status of "diamond delves," "elves'-eyes" and "quickgold" is less clear, and that lack of clarity is a weakness in the poem. However, it is manifest that wind, fire, and dove in lines six and seven manifest Christ in the coming of the Holy Ghost, and even "Maymess" and "March-bloom" hint at the presence of Christ as the common being of the world. Both months are associated with the Blessed Virgin and hence with the Incarnation—March especially because of the feast of the Annunciation. Hence they lend themselves very well to the whole pattern of the poem, for in their "piece-bright" blossoms they anticipate not only a harvest of grain or fruit but of the body and blood of Christ. He is in "May-mess" and "March-bloom" by virtue of His mortal and time-bound flesh (and, consequently, by virtue of the Sacrament), just as He is in the stars by virtue of the epiphany of His glory in the heavenly hosts, just as He is in wind, fire, and dove by virtue of the operation of the Holy Ghost. In short, wherever the persona looks he sees Christ— or, more accurately, he instresses Him—in the heavens above, in the earth and growing things beneath, in the air, fire, and floating things between. Christ's perfect sacrifice is the being of all these things, and it is by discerning the signature of that sacrifice in them (when we instress them) that we discern the unity in their otherwise vast diversity.

In other words the imagery of the poem seems to reflect Hopkins's fundamental metaphysical and theological proposition: that the common being grasped in a confused cognition of a singular substance is, in fact, the very being of Christ; that "all things therefore are charged with love, are charged with God and if we know how to touch them give off sparks and take fire, yield drops [of Christ's blood?] and flow, ring and tell of him" (*SD*, p. 195). As Hillis Miller says, Hopkins achieves a "gradual integration of the world" through his "vision of Christ as the common nature." Because "Christ is the model for all inscapes, and can vibrate simultaneously at all frequencies, He is the ultimate guarantee for the validity of metaphor. It is proper to say that one thing is like another only because all things are like Christ."[31]

Miller's comment is an accurate index of Hopkins's intention in "The Starlight Night" and in most of the "nature poems" between 1876 and 1883. However, a problem remains, and it is one which, so far as I can see, none of Hopkins's critics has confronted. To state it simply: does Hopkins realize his intention in his images or must his readers rely upon his prose for a correct interpretation of the poetry? When I referred to a textbook solution, it was to this difficulty that I alluded; for there is a serious question whether, without the theological works which Father Devlin has edited and interpreted, we could solve the problem of unity in the poems. After we have learned that Hopkins conceives Christ's flesh and blood as the common being of all things, we can understand very easily why stars, doves, and whitebeam constitute a unified pattern or vision. But suppose we had not read the prose and were forced to rely solely upon the poem to disclose its principle of unity. Would it be possible under those circumstances to see what it is that holds Hopkins's world together? Of course the allusions to the saints and to the Holy Ghost would give us some help, but could those conceits, in and of themselves, show us that every instress is literally, not figuratively, of Christ? I rather seriously doubt it, and if I am correct it means we are right back where we began, with the question of what these various inscapes have in common.

The ramifications of the question are far reaching. For one thing, if a proper interpretation of a Hopkins poem requires knowledge of his theological prose, we must conclude that the poem lacks integrity as a work of art. If we must depend for our understanding of an image upon assumptions about

Christology and ontology which are external to the image, we can only say that the image does not really show us what it professes or attempts to show. If perception of a poem's unity depends upon an interpretation of it for which it does not, in itself, offer sufficient grounds, we can only conclude that it lacks unity. Moreover we may press the matter one step further and ask whether, given Hopkins's Newmanized or romanticized Scotism, it is possible for his poems to offer those grounds sufficient for their correct interpretation. One cannot discern in an intuition, *so long as it remains an intuition*, any theological concept whatever; and the latter is precisely what Christ as "Ground of being, and granite of it" is. By the same token an image whose purpose is to convey an intuition cannot also serve to convey a theological or metaphysical definition. Therefore unless the reader has some source of information beyond the metaphoric presentation of the moment of instress, he is not likely to understand either the significance of the particular *visio* or its relationship to other and equally opaque perceptions.

At the present stage in the history of Hopkins criticism the question will probably have to remain moot. We do now have the prose and we have all read it. We know in advance what Hopkins means by his images; therefore it is very difficult to see whether they, in themselves, mean—whether they convey understanding to the reader. Suffice it to say I know of no critic who has discerned Hopkins's intention without recourse to his prose, and given the intuitive nature of his mode of vision it is very difficult to see how it would be possible to do so. By contrast one thinks of Dante's lucid metaphors whose very purpose is to convey conceptual understanding. Dante's universe also has Christ as its principle of unity, and (as we have seen already) its Christological coherence is manifest both in the pattern of the whole and in the minute details which constitute the pattern. Because Dante's metaphors are predicated on abstractive rather than intuitive cognitions he is able to show us not only the thing perceived but also its form or essence, to which God is present innermostly as ground and granite of being. Moreover, because he relies upon a conceptual theology as well as metaphysics, he is also able to show us how all creatures manifest Christ by doing His will and living thereby in His peace. Thus when Christ blazes forth (Dante's brilliantly expressive word is *lampeggiava: Par.,* xiv, 104) from the "fire-folk" in Mars, we require nothing beyond the imagery of the poem to explain or justify the epiphany. Dante represents the saints as stars in a cruciform constellation (*Par.,* xiv, 97–123). It is clear that by the cross, which signifies Christ, the hallowed souls participate in the love which moves the sun and other stars. We understand therefore how it is that saints and stars can both manifest Christ, how he can be their common term.

By taking intuitive experience as the source of his imagery Hopkins precludes for himself the possibility of doing the sort of thing which Dante does. Therefore when Geoffrey Hartman asks how Hopkins "passes from a vivid and immediate sensing to religious insight without rejecting or modifying the former,"[32] I should be inclined to answer that in fact he does not and cannot—that in attempting to do such a thing he has attempted an impossibility. The very nature of human cognition requires that in order to pass to the latter he *must* "modify" the former: by abstracting its form, by uttering the truth of its essence in a concept, and by penetrating to its composite existence in an act of *compositio.* Without those operations of the intellect it is impossible to discern the "religious insight" in an "immediate sensing," and unless the image which conveys the "sensing" carries that discernment with it, it cannot also convey the insight. Aquinas, of course, could have taught Hopkins that, but so for that matter could Scotus: that, at least *pro statu isto,* man cannot rely for knowledge of God on intuitive cognition to the exclusion of conceptual. By resting in the former, in the *visio . . . exsistentis ut exsistens est et ut praesens est videnti secundum suam exsistentiam,*[33] Hopkins renders himself incapable of dealing with the created thing in terms of its essence; and it is only in those terms—and in images which convey the thing in those terms—that one can show Christ shining forth from stars, leaves, or doves. Critics like Devlin and Miller who applaud Hopkins's dwelling on the first act of intellection "to the exclusion of succeeding abstractions," and who maintain that "the *visio existentis ut existens* is the true source of poetry because only this way of seeing things can go behind mere intellectual recognition,"[34] should be more careful about what they are saying. At least they should understand that "intellectual recognition" *must* inform an image if the latter is to manifest the invisible things of God; for those things, by their very nature, are subject to recognition only intellectually. Nor should they forget that in poems whose unity derives from the unity of the experience they convey, "intellectual recognition" is essential to the integrity of the work of art.

Here then is the fundamental weakness in Hopkins's poetry —a failure on the level of the individual poem to achieve the understanding and unity requisite for a poem's meaning and beauty. The brilliant fragments of Hopkins's world fail to cohere because his imagery fails to demonstrate the principle of that coherence. It is only a common participation in Christ that can link saints with stars, and though Hopkins asserts that participation he does not, like Dante, *show* it to us. Because he does not, his poems, though undeniably brilliant, are incomplete. Upon a first reading they move us by sheer force of language. However, when the syntactical excitement fades, we are inclined to feel that we have been deceived—lured into accepting a theological identification which the poem does not earn but merely asserts. Consequently the initial thrill which poems like "The Starlight Night" and "The Windhover" give does not grow into the satisfaction which attends completed wisdom.

Another way to state the same difficulty is to say that we can take little away from a reading of Hopkins save the emotional and verbal experience. His imagery attempts to show us the world in a drop of Christ's blood; and because the mode of perception is wholly dependent upon the sense of ecstasy that it generates, the vision perishes with the language which conveys the ecstasy. Whereas Dante's metaphysical analogies carry intellectual conviction and therefore serve to sustain the emotional force of his metaphors, Hopkins must rely upon his metaphors to persuade us emotionally (since there is nothing in the poem to convince us intellectually) that "natural things, instead of having a derived being, participate directly in the being of the creator"—that they "are not specific symbols, but all mean one thing and the same: the beauty of Christ."[35] These metaphors must show us Christ in "brute beauty" without the aid of concepts, and that, by either Scotist or Thomist standards, is an impossible task. Ecstatic language is not a sufficiently strong glue to hold a poetic universe together; it cannot demonstrate that ours is "a sacred universe"—a world "impregnated to its every fibre with the intimate presence of a God whose supreme actuality preserves it in its own actual existence."

VII

The intent of these remarks is not simply to condemn Hopkins's poetry but rather to point up the predicament of the sacred poet in the modern world. Deprived of access by knowledge to invisible things and yet compelled by his particular muse—indeed by his love of God—to write of those very things, he is forced into eccentricities of vision and into distortions of language. Had Hopkins written as the romantics did of intuitions of created things; and had he either stopped there or at least contented himself with vague intimations of immortality which do not require conceptual definition, his poetry would present no difficulties. The problem (and the interest) stems from his attempt to identify his intuitions with Christ Himself. It is as though Keats had insisted by his use of symbolic language that the being of the nightingale was the very blood of the Passion and his own ecstasy a communion with Christ in the bird's song. The idea is outrageous, but that is precisely the kind of identification that Hopkins attempts. He tries to force experience to yield what only knowledge can give; and since he attempts the impossible we should not be surprised that he fails.

On the other hand the very failure has its interest for us. By stretching intuition to its epistemological limits Hopkins exhausts its possibilities. The poems from 1876 to 1883 cannot be duplicated. In their own particular line no one can go further, and it is clear that Hopkins, even by going to the end of that line, could not go far enough to meet the demands of a sacred subject. One consequence of his falling short is the weakness of the poems themselves; another is the desolation of the later and radically different poetry. For the very source of terror in those "terrible sonnets" is the failure of the original power of confused cognition. When the intuition fails, Christ's sacrifice is no longer visible in the creation; the poet as a consequence finds himself in a state of isolation that is almost literally a hell. With Newman he looks "into this living busy world, and see[s] no reflexion of its Creator" (*Ap.,* p. 216); and he cannot bear the sight. Hopkins's various descriptions of that unbearable isolation—"cliffs of fall / Frightful, sheer, no-man-fathomed" ("No Worst, There is None")—constitute the finest poetry he wrote. However, it is essentially a poetry of private, psychological experience, not sacred poetry. In fact its very existence testifies to the terrifying impossibility of having God and the keen delight of that possession—and consequently to the impossibility of sacred poetry—in a world which substitutes real assent for notional.

5
Eliot and
Mystical Wisdom

As we turn from Hopkins to Eliot—specifically to the *Four Quartets*—it is well to distinguish at the outset between the experience which a poem interprets and the interpretation which the poem gives. In Hopkins's case for instance, whatever we may think of the intuitional, Scotist imagery of his poetry, we are none the less struck by the fact of a vivid experience which the imagery seeks to convey. In the poems with which we have been primarily concerned, those written between 1876 and 1883, Hopkins is, above all else, seeking to convince us of an experience of God's presence which seems to flame out of the physical creation. It is clearly the poet's sense of that presence which kindles the verbal energy characteristic of these works, and though we may object to the inexact metaphors and to the disunity which results from that imprecision, we can scarcely gainsay the emotional force of the language and imagery. Indeed we are persuaded by that very force of the validity of the experience which lies back of it, and I am rather inclined to think that it is that persuasion which gives Hopkins's work its undeniable strength and freshness. Though we may feel that Hopkins does not do justice in metaphor to his sacred subject, the sheer excitement of the poetry convinces us that the subject is authentic—some taste of God Himself, of His power, beauty, and sweetness, which seems to have its source in the dazzling variety of His creatures.

Eliot's mature poetry also concerns itself with an experience of the ineffable. Over and again he alludes to "moments of illumination," moments in the rose garden when one is looking into the heart of light, moments when music is heard so deeply that "you are the music / While the music lasts." The longer one contemplates the *Quartets* the more convinced he becomes that the poems were written solely to interpret that moment of intersection of the timeless with time. In fact Eliot says as much on several occasions, and whatever the context of the particular statement may be, the point is always the same:

> the sudden illumination—
> We had the experience but missed the meaning,
> And approach to the meaning restores the experience
> In a different form, beyond any meaning
> We can assign to happiness.   ("The Dry Salvages," ii)

It is that approach to the meaning and the consequent restoration of the experience in another form which these remarkable poems attempt, with a great measure of success, to convey.

To say as much may be a critical truism; but it is important to make the point in the present context, for it is that restoration of the experience in approach to its meaning which distinguishes Eliot's poetry from Hopkins's. Indeed, Eliot in the *Quartets* is supremely concerned with meaning, and if we ask why he was more successful than Hopkins in conveying an ineffable experience in poetic metaphor, we should answer by saying that he came to understand the meaning of that experience far better than Hopkins ever did. By virtue of that understanding—as we shall see presently—he distinguished the experience as such from its concomitant circumstances and discovered that its locus was not the physical creation at all but the human soul. He discovered, in other words, that it was an authentic mystical experience, not an intuition of God in created things; and between the two there is a very great difference indeed. The latter might be said to fall short of the precision of metaphysics and theology; the former transcends that precision. The latter offers itself as an alternative to knowledge; the former as a mode of apprehension transcending but not effacing knowledge. The latter seems to be linked invariably to some form of an idealist epistemology which finds the material world unintelligible and which seeks therefore for a substitute for concepts abstracted from phantasms. The former accepts the fact of the creation's intelligibility and of the validity of concepts, but it attempts to reach beyond concepts to a direct experience of God in the soul. Unlike intuition or confused cognition, mystical experience is not a retreat from the presumed evils of conceptual cognition but a transcendence of its goodness. That is why Maritain says that in the mystical wisdom of St. John of the Cross "we are . . . at the antipodes of neo-Platonic intellectualism . . . at the very heart of the theology of St. Thomas."[1]

If Maritain is correct, it means that by pursuing the negative way of *Dark Night of the Soul* and *Ascent of Mount Carmel* Eliot, by a route very different from Dante's, comes to an intellectual position which is compatible with Dante's. It also means that though the *Quartets* are predicated on the experience of God rather than upon knowledge of Him, their symbolic vision, though distinct from, is in no way hostile to conceptual cognition. We must therefore understand precisely what Maritain is saying, and the starting point for doing so is a firm grasp of the following proposition: that the locus of mystical experience is the will rather than the intellect. St. Thomas offers a clear distinction between the activities of those two faculties: "the movement of the appetitive power is towards things in respect of their own condition, whereas the act of a cognitive power follows the mode of the knower" (*ST*, II [2], 27, 4). It is into the former movement that charity is infused; into the latter, faith. The experience of that infused charity in the former brings the mystic into union with God; the conceptual understanding of infused faith in the latter gives the theologian a science of God. Consequently we can say that charity apprehends God in an experience of Him as He is in His "own condition," faith in a knowledge of Him which is according to "the mode of the knower." Between the two virtues, their proper faculties, and their corresponding wisdoms the difference is so considerable that there cannot possibly be conflict, confusion, or mutual exclusion.

Therefore we may reasonably say that the very distinctness

of the two wisdoms makes it possible for them to complement one another. That is why Maritain insists upon the harmony between St. Thomas and St. John: the former is the master of theological wisdom, "the Doctor *par excellence* of the *speculatively* practical science of contemplation and of union with God"; the latter is the master of mystical wisdom, "the pre-eminent Doctor of the *practically* practical science of contemplation and union with God." St. Thomas, in other words, is a "demonstrator," St. John a "practitioner of wisdom," but neither may scorn nor dispense with the other. The practice of wisdom is a higher vocation than its demonstration, for the former is not a "question of merely learning, but rather of suffering divine things . . . of knowing God by experience."[2] On the other hand mystical wisdom cannot supplant theological wisdom (as intuition attempts to do) because, as we now see, the two are quite literally "planted" in different faculties of the soul. Indeed mystical experience can no more offer itself as a substitute for conceptual theology than charity can offer itself as a substitute for faith. Their very distinctness preserves the integrity of each and therefore their ultimate harmony.

Moreover that harmony is insured by the fact that "knowing God by experience" also, though in a fashion quite different from theology's, requires the operation of concepts. "They are not suppressed, for that would be contrary to the very nature of our intellect which needs them to be in act." What happens is that "distinct concepts are all silent . . . and the confused concepts which intervene, and which can remain quite unperceived, play only a material [as opposed to a formal] role." They cease in other words to be a formal means of knowing as they are in metaphysical and theological wisdoms, for in mystical wisdom charity plays the formal part and the experience, the suffering of God, "passes through [the concepts] without being measured by them."[3] Nevertheless their very presence binds experience to demonstration and supports Maritain's principal thesis—that mystical experience, though higher than metaphysical and theological knowledges, transcends them without obliterating them. Therefore he can argue convincingly that there is no contradiction between the doctrine of St. Thomas and that of St. John of the Cross.

But how, precisely, does charity provide an experience of God? What happens exactly when charity becomes the form of divine knowledge and the concepts merely the matter of that cognition? Maritain, drawing on both St. Thomas and St. John of the Cross, explains that "it is proper to the gift of wisdom to make use of . . . infused charity, in order to make it pass, under the special inspiration of the Holy Ghost, to the status of an *objective medium* of knowledge (*objectum quo* in scholastic terminology)." In other words charity in mystical wisdom plays the same role that the *species impressa* plays in metaphysical wisdom; it is the intention of the thing known in the knower by which a real union of the two is effected, by which truth is made possible. However, in this case, given the nature of the intention of God as divine charity, the union is not expressed in concept but is suffered, so to speak, in the very center of the soul. Therefore, as Maritain says, when we experience charity "we not only experience our love for God, but it is God Himself whom we experience by our love."[4]

However, we must not forget that that experience comes in support rather than in default of knowledge; and to illustrate the relationship between the wisdoms we can scarcely do better than to look again at what happens to Dante when he comes to the vision of God. He sees, we recall, three circles, the second signifying God the Son. Then upon it he sees imposed the likeness of a man, signifying the Incarnation. At first he is thwarted in his effort to understand this "impossible union of spheres of existence"—*come si convenne / l'imago al cerchio e come vi s'indova* (how the image was fitted to the circle and how it has its place there). Indeed he never does *understand* it, but he does enter into it when mystical wisdom comes to complete theological knowledge. His mind, he says, was smitten *da un fulgore in che sua voglia venne* (by a flash wherein came its wish). The wish is granted when the concept ceases to be the form and becomes merely the matter of experience; when charity, *l'amor che move il sole e l'altre stelle,* moves Dante's will and presumably becomes for him the very experience of God; when the knowledge of God is transcended, but not effaced, by the suffering of God (*Par.,* xxxiii, 137–45). At that culminating moment in the *Comedy,* at the moment when mystical wisdom carries Dante beyond theology, he finds himself "at the very heart of the theology of St. Thomas."

It becomes clear from these remarks how radically mystical experience differs from intuition or confused cognition. Intuition, whatever its exact epistemological status, must finally be regarded as a mode of knowledge. We have spoken of it as "experience," and in comparison with conceptual cognition, on account of its affective nature, it seems to be. On the other hand it is quite clear that intuition is an activity of the intellect rather than of the will and has as its object knowledge (however vague) rather than passion or union. That is why Hopkins was clearly mistaken in trying to deal with an authentic experience of God—I am assuming it was that—in terms of intuition. By doing so he bound himself to a grasp of God according to the mode of the knower rather than *"according to a mode that is suprahuman and supernatural."*[5] Consequently he was forced to seek (and to represent in image) the blood of Christ and the fire of the Spirit in his apprehension of other creatures rather than where he might have sought it more profitably, in the activities of his own will infused with divine charity. He evidently failed to recognize that what he suffered was by its very nature impervious to cognition whether confused or distinct, incapable of apprehension either real or notional; that it belonged to an entirely different order of spiritual activity whose end is union with God, not as He is known but as He is. One is inclined to believe that Hopkins should have taken St. John rather than Scotus for his mentor, and the fact that Eliot was able to understand and interpret the experience of God for what it was and to recognize its locus in the will is almost certainly a consequence of his devotion to the Spanish mystic.

II

But how fully, in fact, *did* Eliot understand these matters? Are we not making exorbitant claims? We must be frank to admit that he did not make the distinction between mysticism and intuition in so many words; therefore we cannot say that he made it in quite the explicit way we have set it forth here. On the other hand we do know that he was interested in Maritain's work, and it is not impossible that he had read the very discussion of mystical wisdom on which we have predicated our distinction. Moreover there can be no question that when he read St. John of the Cross he did so against an intellectual background that was strongly colored by scepticism and consequently by the substitution of intuition for abstraction and conception. He was, like Hopkins, an inheritor of the romantic tradition in art and poetry (indeed the French symbolists from whom he learned so much might well be regarded as taking the anti-intellectual strain in romanticism to its logical and possibly absurd conclusion). Moreover what he learned from F. H. Bradley, whose doctrine of "immediate experience" is a version of intuitive cognition, could only have accentuated that tendency; and his conversion to Anglo-Catholicism placed him squarely in the antimetaphysical tradition of Newman and the Catholic revival.[6] Against the backdrop of such influences, St. John's mysticism, rooted in Aquinas's intellectualism, must have stood out in sharp contrast.

That much is conjecture, but there is firm evidence that even before his conversion Eliot had distinguished, with Aquinas's help, between intuition and "intelligence" and had spoken out very clearly in favor of the latter. I refer to a debate in *The Criterion* in 1927 which was initiated by Middleton Murry's repudiation of Thomism in favor of a new synthesis based on intuition.[7] In his contribution to that debate Eliot declares himself to be " 'on the side of what we call the intelligence.' " He does not "wish to expunge the word 'intuition' from the dictionary," but he refuses to make a generic distinction between intuition and conceptual knowledge or to appeal to the former at the expense of the latter. He also tells us that though he does not know a great deal about Aquinas he has read works by Gilson and Maritain and "here and there" in the *Summa* itself. With his characteristic deference —"I am not yet certain to what point I should wish to champion the 'system' of St. Thomas"—he does, in fact, champion it against Murry's scepticism and appeal to intuition.[8] Eliot does not mention mystical wisdom in this context,[9] but it is difficult to imagine how a man of his perspicacity, who had examined in some detail the relationship between intuitive and conceptual cognition, who had decided in favor of the latter, and who had done so with specific reference to Thomist theology, could have failed to see where St. John's mystical wisdom stands in relationship to these categories. Though he may never have said to himself in so many words that by practicing the doctrine of St. John of the Cross he would set himself free from the modern confusion of experience and knowledge and come "to the very heart of the theology of St. Thomas," he must surely have seen that St. John's mysticism, unlike intuition but very much like St. Thomas's theology and metaphysics, is " 'on the side of what we call the intelligence.' "

III

A fundamental reason for that alliance—one which is implicit in Maritain's comparison of the two theologians—is that both of them believe in the authenticity of knowledge abstracted from sense experience of an intelligible creation. It requires only a moment's reflection to recognize that that fact is of considerable importance to our present discussion. Poetry invariably takes the physical creation, directly or indirectly, at its point of departure and is therefore in some degree determined by the poet's attitude toward that creation. We might expect a mystic like St. John to distrust the validity of sense impressions and to be sceptical about the goodness and intelligibility of the "living busy world." We might think that because of the profoundly interior nature of mystical experience he would have more in common epistemologically with Newman or Hopkins than with Aquinas or Dante. However, in this regard, as in his clear distinction between knowledge and experience, he is more nearly a thirteenth than a nineteenth or twentieth-century Catholic.

Consider the passage near the beginning of *Ascent of Mount Carmel* in which he explains that mortification of the senses leaves the soul in "the darkness of night" because "the soul, as soon as God infuses it into the body, is like a smooth, blank board upon which nothing is painted; and, save for that which it experiences through the senses, nothing is communicated to it, in the course of nature, from any other source."[10] Here is the fundamental proposition of Thomist epistemology, and it stands in radical contradiction to the general bias of idealist epistemology which seems always to underlie theories of intuitive cognition. Idealism, because it doubts the intelligibility of the physical creation, distrusts the evidence of the senses and the concepts drawn from them; consequently it turns to intuition. St. John builds his mystical theology on the assumption that the soul, at least in this life, *can* acquire knowledge by abstraction from sense perception *and in no other way.* In fact, it is on account of that capacity that denial of sense perception contributes to the purgation of the soul. He admonishes the disciples of the negative way to mortify the senses, not because they are unreliable or deceptive in their epistemological function, but because the experience of God as charity in the soul is generically distinct from the sciences of God derived by abstraction. Such mortification may resemble very closely the mortification which scepticism requires and which issues in an intuitional epistemology, but its motive and its consequence are totally different. The two may look alike, but, to vary Eliot's image, they do not grow in the same hedgerow.

A man who had studied the rival claims of intuition and conceptual knowledge, who had read "here and there" in the *Summa,* and who had immersed himself so deeply in the work of St. John that the latter's language had become his own, can

scarcely have failed to recognize that distinction. We are
therefore not surprised that Eliot's imagery of the physical
creation reflects that recognition. Consider how radically his
treatment of the *res extra animam* differs from Hopkins's. For
the latter, as we know, the physical object exists primarily in
order to release the fire of the Spirit or the blood of Christ.
Mistaking the physical creation for the source of his experi-
ence of God causes Hopkins to treat that creation primarily as
a vehicle for the experience. I realize that many of Hopkins's
readers will dissent from that proposition, insisting on the
contrary that he is profoundly committed to sensible experi-
ence of physical things. On one level, of course, he is; but it
is also obvious from his imagery that his commitment does
not extend to the quiddity of those things. Rather he is so much
concerned to grasp Christ in a confused cognition of them
that he evades the question of what they are in their own right
as existing substances. Upon reading his poems, we in turn
are much less interested in the falcon than in the fire of
Christ's stress which he releases in the poet's subjective ap-
prehension of him; much less concerned with the stars or the
whitebeam than with Christ's flaring out of them (or at least
seeming to do so) when the persona of the sonnet instresses
them.

In this respect, as in so many others, Hopkins seems to re-
semble Newman, who consistently regards the physical crea-
tion as an economy or symbol of God rather than as a reality
in its own right. As early as 1834 Newman was prepared, if
not to question the existence of matter, at least to "deny that
what we saw was more than accidents of it";[11] and in 1861 he
goes so far as to suggest that in our inability to know the
quiddity of anything, we must be content with phenomena.
Since he can discern no necessary connection between those
phenomena and their causes, Newman proceeds to advance the
altogether remarkable suggestion that the thing we call a rose
"may be an Angel; it may be the soul of a child; it may be
. . . one of the innumerable (immediate) acts of the . . .
Creator Himself." Indeed, Newman adds, "there is nothing

absurd or impossible in the idea . . . that what we call mat-
ter, that is, the (hidden) cause of the phenomena which we
receive through the senses, is simply and nothing else but
. . . (a divine) action, mediately, or immediately" (*Note-
book,* II, 208). There is only one short step from that last
adverb to an assertion that every so-called "thing" our senses
perceive is the immediate presence of Christ-in-sacrifice, re-
quiring only intuition for its manifestation. The thing, no mat-
ter how much one emphasizes its distinctive scape or stress,
is not finally important as a creature but as a phenomenologi-
cal presentation of divine being. Hopkins's famous appeal to
thisness at the expense of *whatness* must be regarded, para-
doxically, as a sceptic's evasion of the thing in its own sub-
stantial existence and intelligibility.

In the imagery of Eliot's *Quartets* the *res extra animam*
retains its identity; and that fact is of profound importance
for our understanding of those poems. It is in their images, in
the very shape and structure of the metaphor, that Eliot re-
stores the experience in an approach to its meaning, and those
images are predicated on the existence of the *res.* Their mean-
ing—and hence the meaning of the ineffable experience which
they convey—might even be said to be defined by the persona's
attitude toward the physical object. We can best define that
attitude by saying that it differs from Hopkins's in the very
way in which the mystic's approach to the creature differs from
the sceptic's, and from Dante's in the way the mystic's ap-
proach differs from the metaphysician's or theologian's. In
other words we may define Eliot's attitude—which is to say
that we may characterize his imagery—by saying that it reflects
the view of the creation set forth in the work of St. John of
the Cross. The imagery of the *Quartets* depicts a world of real
substances which are manifestly good and (so far as we can
discern) intelligible in their own right but which, in contrast
with the soul's experience of God in charity, are of no conse-
quence whatever. That is precisely the way in which the au-
thentic Christian mystic regards the physical creation; and it
is no exaggeration to say that Eliot's imagery gives us what he

never gave in prose statement—evidence that he understood the nature of mystical wisdom.[12]

There is for instance the way in which he deals with the individual, composite substance. The act of knowledge necessarily addresses itself to the thing—to the quiddity of the thing if it be true knowing such as Dante's or to the thing *sicut est in se* if it be intuitive cognition of Hopkins's sort. That Eliot in the *Quartets* is concerned with mystical experience rather than with cognition of either kind seems to be indicated by the fact that at no point in these poems does the *res* become the object of attention—either in respect of its quiddity as a subject for abstraction or in respect of its existence and individuality as a subject for real apprehension or instress. Rather its purpose is to point, sometimes directly, sometimes by negation or contrast, to an experience whose locus is not the external world but the human soul. In the landscapes of the *Quartets* the thing, as thing, is present in its full substantiality and frequently in great beauty. It is not to be denied or ignored, but neither is it to attract very much attention. The rose of the *Quartets* is still a rose—not an Angel, not the soul of a child, not "one of the . . . innumerable (immediate) acts of the . . . (Ever-present) Creator Himself." However, we are concerned neither with its nature, with the form of the rose, as Dante would be, nor with its susceptibility to intuition. Consequently we can neither derive knowledge of God from it in Dante's Thomistic fashion nor, in Hopkins's, smell God in its sweetness. Rather we must use it as an "objective correlative" for the soul's experience of God's sweetness, which is not knowledge but charity and which, in mystical illumination, He communicates directly rather than through the medium of creatures.

The consequence for Eliot's imagery is a curious mixture of exact detail and surrealistic fantasy. As one enters the rose garden at the beginning of "Burnt Norton," he quickly becomes aware that things *extra animam* have existence but that they are, comparatively speaking, of no importance. The shrubbery, the roses, the alley, the box circle, the drained pool with its dry concrete and brown edges impress their substantial existence upon us; yet at the same time they threaten to disappear in the autumn heat shimmer. It is as though the soul's experience—signified by the unheard laughter, the unseen eyebeams, the water out of sunlight, the guests—were on the point of blotting out these physical things; yet the blotting never quite takes place. As a result the poetry hangs suspended precisely where Eliot says it should—at the point of intersection of the timeless with time. In fact Eliot leaves us with the distinct impression that if the bird had not said "go," that if the illumination had lasted an instant longer (though, as he warns us, we cannot speak temporally), the physical creation would have vanished from sight. However, since "human kind / Cannot bear very much reality," the spell is broken, water "out of heart of light" vanishes, and we are left, presumably, with the dry concrete of physical experience—what, from the vantage of mystical experience, seems to be "the waste sad time / Stretching before and after" ("Burnt Norton," i, v).

Compared with water out of sunlight the dry pool is dull indeed, and Eliot admits that dullness fully. However, he does not so much as hint that the physical thing is a mere illusion. Rather it is always there, it is what it is, and it directs us to the soul's experience which, though totally different from it, never effaces it. The thing does not reduce itself to a symbol or what Newman would call an economy of the invisible world; it does not buckle in order to release the fire of Christ's stress. Rather, like the things of Dante's world, it remains itself; only, unlike Dante's things, its purpose, from first to last, is to direct us to an experience which, because it is genuinely mystical, is totally unrelated to the thing. Therefore we may say that the things of this world do not matter in Eliot's imagery provided we remember that the standard for measuring their value is mystical rather than ontological.

IV

Neither, says Eliot, does poetry matter. The mystical context of that statement serves to interpret it, and it is only in that context that the statement is true. Had Newman said it—in the context of his epistemological idealism and scepticism—we should have been compelled to discount it for the very same reason that we discount Plato's distrust of poets. Had Hopkins said it, we should likewise be forced to gainsay it (and it may not be wholly unfair to interpret his deliberate distortion of syntax as a tacit admission of poetry's inadequacy in respect of the subject matter of intuition). Unless one is talking about genuine mystical experience, it is incorrect to say that our apprehension of God transcends utterance in words and images. However, if one *is* talking about genuine mystical experience as Eliot seems to be, it is no offence to poetry to say that it does not matter. Indeed we might say that the only alternative to poetry's complete adequacy as an utterance of things known is its utter inadequacy to express an experience of God which transcends knowledge. To say, in the latter context, that poetry does not matter is analogous to saying, in the same context, that the physical creation does not matter. Neither the mystery of the existence of *things* and of God's presence in them nor the adequacy of such poetry as Dante's to convey a science of that mystery and that presence is in any way contradicted by one's introducing another kind of mystery and another kind of presence which make different requirements of the intellect and of language.

Eliot leaves us no doubt as to the context of his statement about poetry. He has told us already, in the fifth section of "Burnt Norton," that "Words, after speech, reach / Into the silence," and the silence in that particular context obviously signifies the divine illumination. In short, Eliot is saying that words, because they move in time, are insufficient to express an experience of that which is timeless, to "reach / The stillness." If we have that passage in mind, we should be suspicious, immediately, when we encounter the veritable rash of words, the profusion of "poetic" poetry, with which the second part of "East Coker" begins. Moreover in the opening section of this second quartet we have seen those who "keep time" go into the darkness, and dawn point to silence—the same dark-

ness and silence which, "Burnt Norton" tells us, words will not
be able to express. Therefore we should recognize that the
question "What is the late November doing?" is not a serious
attempt to convey the subject but rather that it is a parody of
another kind of poetry which conveys (or once conveyed) an-
other kind of subject. Eliot's lines might be regarded as a
deliberately bad imitation of poetry such as Gloucester's "late
eclipses in the sun and moon." Eliot is saying that what hap-
pens in old age is not "what one had expected," and given the
medieval and renaissance conviction that all creatures exist in
a metaphysical harmony, it would be perfectly reasonable to
speak of the disturbances which interrupt old age in terms of
seasonal and cosmic disturbances. As we have seen from a
study of the *Comedy,* such analogies are more than figures of
speech, for they are predicated on the analogy of being. How-
ever, such language will work to convey truth only in the order
of metaphysical and theological concept—not in the order
of mystical experience. The latter has nothing to do—at least
nothing directly to do—with the things which revolve in
space; consequently it is oblivious to analogies between the
seasons of the year and the seasons of the soul.

Given the mystical assumptions of the *Quartets,* Eliot is per-
fectly justified in parodying the stock metaphors and the pat-
tern of concepts which they imply. He is even justified in say-
ing that the "knowledge derived from experience / . . . im-
poses a pattern, and falsifies, / For the pattern is new in every
moment / And every moment is a new and shocking / Valua-
tion of all we have been" ("East Coker," ii). That is true be-
cause the moment of which Eliot speaks is one of experience
in the soul rather than of conceptual understanding abstracted
from things and from the "pattern" of things. Hence we may
say that when Eliot dismisses his "periphrastic study in a worn-
out poetical fashion," he in effect exchanges the wisdoms of
Dante and Aquinas for that of St. John of the Cross. However,
one must not forget—and the imagery indicates that Eliot did
not—that between the two there is no mutual exclusion. It is
rather that whereas for the former words are adequate to ex-

press concepts of the true, for the latter words can only point to the silence, the stillness, in which the true is experienced in itself.

The opening passage of "Little Gidding" is a good example of how words and things may serve to point to that which is not in things and which cannot be uttered in words. The key phrase here is "the heart's heat," by which Eliot signifies the locus and nature of the experience of fire:

> When the short day is brightest, with frost and fire,
> The brief sun flames the ice, on pond and ditches,
> In windless cold that is the heart's heat.
>
> ("Little Gidding," i)

The juxtaposition of phrases in the last line might almost be regarded as a key to all the imagery in the *Quartets,* for it makes us see vividly that the *where* of the stillness is nowhere and that its when is not in time. The heat of the flame on the ice is a spiritual heat which the heart experiences and whose source is not the sun but the Holy Ghost—"pentecostal fire." In fact the relationship between "windless cold" and "heart's heat" is analogous to that between the dry concrete pool and "water out of sunlight," for in each instance the experience of the Spirit in the soul is represented in images which both point to that experience and at the same time suggest the radical distinction between the experience itself and the words or things which attempt to convey it. Nothing could be less like the experience of God than a dry pool or a frozen pond or ditch. The words do convey the qualities of stillness, brilliance, suddenness, and transience which are characteristic of the moment of illumination, but Eliot uses these words so deftly that in the very process of conveying those qualities they confess their incapacity to do more than reach into silence. We are not allowed to forget that "midwinter spring" is nothing more than an accident of climate and, though a vehicle in the poetry for the "sempiternal," that it will be "sodden towards sundown." Earth, water, air, and fire in fortunate conjunction yield a moment of midwinter beauty which serves as a metaphor for the heart's heat of charity, the experience of the living flame of love. However, earth, water, air, and fire, and the words which express them as metaphor, do not matter. Eliot holds before us both the absolute necessity of things and words and their absolute inconsequence in comparison with the suffering of divine things.

Were one to confuse the experience of God with the experience of temporal things, he would be forced in the end (if, indeed, he is to come to the stillness) to acknowledge his mistake. "If you came this way in may time, you would find the hedges / White again, in May, with voluptuary sweetness." However, whether you come by day (May), thinking you know what you are coming for or by night (midwinter?), "like a broken king," who knows, we infer, that he does not know, "it would be the same at the end of the journey." The former is Hopkins's way—one recalls the voluptuary sweetness of "Spring," of "Pied Beauty," of "Hurrahing in Harvest." One also recalls the end of the journey in the "terrible sonnets"—what Eliot here calls "the world's end." Indeed the experience of pentecostal fire, of the Holy Ghost, is exactly that, the end of the world, of all created things; for the stillness is not in time's covenant. Therefore Eliot is saying it is better for us to be disabused from the very beginning of our journey: to know that what appears to be everlasting and which can even serve to signify God's holy fire in metaphor will not last the afternoon. Blossoms of snow are more nearly adequate images of the ineffable than the darling buds of May, for while the former must necessarily point beyond themselves, the latter may distract us from the world's end and lead us to confuse the sweetness of God with the sweetness of his creatures, the piece-bright paling with "Christ and his mother and all his hallows." Dante and Aquinas knew better: that the role of sweet things is not to convey an *experience* of divine sweetness but rather to lead us to God by serving as a source of concepts. Eliot knew better too—that the experience of the sweetness is in the soul and has nothing to do with things; he was not himself—at least not in the *Quartets*—concerned with concepts.

V

In light of these considerations it seems reasonable to say that Eliot's keen delight and the poetry which is its consequence, though radically different from Dante's, is finally compatible with the latter's traditional theology and metaphysics. Dante delights in the *knowledge* of God, both natural and revealed; Eliot delights in the *experience* of Him. The two modes of delight are radically different from one another, yet they complement each other. By following the theology of St. John of the Cross, Eliot, whether consciously or not, came to a vision of the world that is altogether compatible with Dante's Thomism.

By understanding that fact and the way in which Eliot conveys his vision in the imagery of the *Quartets,* we put ourselves in a position to account for an aspect of those poems which many critics, even sympathetic ones, have found objectionable. I refer to what Denis Donoghue calls Eliot's "Manicheanism": "The redemption of time will be his theme, his case, but he will have to resist a Manichean force within himself which is notoriously subversive; it doesn't really believe that time can be redeemed, it fears that the human scale of action is puny, beyond or beneath redemption." Donoghue alludes specifically to "certain moments in the *Quartets* when Eliot couldn't quite convince himself of human value, and even the pretty, inoffensive things are voided and cleared away before they can be redeemed." Such is the case with the "poor dancers" of "East Coker":

> Keeping time,
> Keeping the rhythm in their dancing
> As in their living in the living seasons
> The time of the seasons and the constellations
> The time of milking and the time of harvest

The time of the coupling of man and woman
And that of beasts. Feet rising and falling.
Eating and drinking. Dung and death.

"It is a gruff dismissal," says Donoghue, "and it points to the deepest embarrassment . . . in Eliot's poetry; the feeling, in part, that all the declared values of human life are somehow illusory and, in part, that nevertheless God so loved the world that He gave up for its redemption His beloved Son." Between the two propositions there appears to be an obvious discrepancy—one which Donoghue does not feel that Eliot resolves. He approves of Eliot's purposes but wishes "that they were charged with an even warmer sense of human value in all its limitation." He wishes that the *Quartets* "were a more Franciscan poem."[13]

I am inclined to think that the objection loses its force when we understand Eliot's motive for renunciation. One may renounce the world because he is a Manichean, but if our analysis of the *Quartets* is correct, that is clearly not Eliot's reason for doing so. All we really need do in order to understand the radical asceticism of the *Quartets* is to remember that from first to last the standard of value for measuring "even the pretty, inoffensive things" is mystical rather than theological or metaphysical. It is not hard to remember that; the very texture of the imagery makes it hard to forget. Once we allow that imagery to cast its spell upon us, once we take its quality seriously, we cannot miss the reality and beauty and goodness of the physical creation. Neither, of course, can we miss perceiving the radically different kind of beauty and goodness which pertains to the holy and, in comparison with which, the world fades into insignificance. Moreover, if we allow that latter beauty to possess us, I believe we shall be convinced that the "echoed ecstasy" is sufficiently compelling to justify "the agony / Of death and birth" ("East Coker," iii). We shall be convinced that Eliot "despises" earthly things (if, indeed, we can use that word) for the very reason that St. John of the Cross despised them—not because those things are evil, illusory, or unintelligible, but because, by darkening "the desires and faculties with respect to these *good* things . . . the interior motions and acts of the soul may come to be moved by God divinely."[14]

Eliot said as much himself in a letter to Bonamy Dobrée in 1936. Dobrée expressed "horror" at the epigraph from St. John to *Sweeney Agonistes:* "Hence the soul cannot be possessed of the divine union, until it has divested itself of the love of created beings." Eliot responds that St. John's statement is "not for you and me, but for people seriously engaged in pursuing the Way of Contemplation. It is only to be read in relation to that Way: i.e., merely to kill one's human affections will get one nowhere, it would be only to become rather more a completely living corpse than most people are."[15] How seriously Eliot was himself engaged in pursuing the way of contemplation I do not know; his "you and me" may simply be good manners. In any event I believe we may say with conviction the *Quartets* demonstrate a clear understanding of that Way and that, like St. John's statement, they are "only to be read in relation to that Way." Their purpose is to render in image that "condition of complete simplicity" which is the property of mystical wisdom because it costs "not less than everything" ("Little Gidding," v). However, the poetry does not forget that in paying everything for that simplicity one still affirms the goodness, the intelligibility of the things which one pays. The *Quartets* do not, save in a few moments of weakness, despise the physical creature save as an obstacle to the achievement of divine simplicity.

VI

It would perhaps be only fair to mention some of those moments of weakness—and not only fair but instructive; for the weaknesses of the *Quartets* are so closely allied to their strengths that the former serve, by contrast, to define the latter. Two such instances of weakness come to mind immediately, in both of which, though in different ways, Eliot confuses mystical wisdom with conceptual cognition. I refer to the generally acknowledged inferiority of "The Dry Salvages" and to what I should call the "bad politics," the "historicism," of "Little Gidding."

In the former the line which serves as a key to the meaning of the poem commits the error of confusing the wisdoms in a most blatant way: "The hint half guessed, the gift half understood, is Incarnation" (v). "The hint . . . the gift" is the moment of illumination—the moment in the rose garden, the midwinter spring. In the other poems Eliot is content that words should do no more than point to the ineffable; here he insists on defining the experience in terms of theological concept. It is precisely Hopkins's procedure: to evoke an experience and then to impose theological definition upon it. It is not simply that the definition is unjust or invalid but rather that, being a definition, a notion, it belongs to a different order of things from that which we call experience. The science of theology does offer an explanation for the sources of mystical experience in terms of the doctrine of the Incarnation; but the experience itself, as experience, cannot be said to *be* "Incarnation." The restoration of the experience in an approach to its meaning requires us to keep meaning and experience distinct. Eliot in this instance blurs the two to the detriment of the poetry.

The blurring is characteristic of "The Dry Salvages" as a whole. Nowhere else in the *Quartets* does Eliot bore us with generalizations and definitions; nor would they be boring here if they sprang from a conceptual or scientific wisdom. They bore because they do not carry conviction, and they fail to carry conviction because they are pasted upon a mode of perception which transcends conception and definition. Though Hugh Kenner's approach to the *Quartets* is radically different from that which we are taking here, he puts his finger directly on the problem with which we are concerned. He refers to Eliot's statement

> I have said before
> That the past experience revived in the meaning
> Is not the experience of one life only
> But of many generations.   ("Dry Salvages," ii)

"He has *not*," remarks Kenner, "said this before: it has said itself, with unselfconscious authority." He proceeds to quote from "East Coker":

> a lifetime burning in every moment
> And not the lifetime of one man only
> But of old stones that cannot be deciphered.

The latter passage catches the drama of an experience of the ineffable which transcends conceptualization; the former passage, by trying to reduce mystical illumination to the language of concept, becomes tiresomely and unconvincingly pedantic. In Kenner's words, the former is a "leaden paraphrase" of the latter; it uses "poetic illumination . . . as a datum in a labored construction."[16] However, we must not forget that all "construction" in poetry need not be labored and that concept and definition can carry conviction when the mode of illumination is metaphysical or theological. In that circumstance the construction is not a paraphrase but an original utterance.

The flaw in "Little Gidding" is the exact opposite of that in "The Dry Salvages." Whereas in the latter Eliot allows conceptual definition to obscure the mystical experience to which it alludes, in the former he allows the dramatic force of the experience to usurp the authority of the concept. I refer to Eliot's insistence that his visit to a place symbolic of anti-puritan sentiment, of Catholic and royalist resistance, is "not to ring the bell backward"; that

> We cannot revive old factions
> We cannot restore old policies
> Or follow an antique drum.

Rather we must recognize that puritans and royalists alike

> Accept the constitution of silence
> And are folded in a single party.

The key word is *silence;* it is presumably that same silence to which words can reach only "after speech" and in comparison with which the words do not matter. The implication of the entire passage is that like things or words or poetry, parties—political and ecclesiastical commitments and alignments—do not matter. Their purpose, like the purpose of words, is to point to the ineffable stillness, to be "a symbol perfected in death" ("Little Gidding," iii).

Again the problem is of perspective; things or words or politics matter or do not matter depending on the standard by which they are measured. From the point of view of mystical wisdom, in contrast with the experience of the night of God, no human thing is significant. However, to proceed as Eliot does here to a rather rough and ready dismissal of intellectual convictions about the right and wrong of political positions and human events is, in effect, to confuse the demands which mystical wisdom imposes with the equally strict, though distinct, requirements of theology, politics, and ethics. It is, in Allen Tate's phrase, to take the "long view" of history in which we lose sight of particular things and human values,[17] and it lays Eliot open to criticism of the sort which Donoghue directs against him. That is why we may say that the error here is a mirror image of that in "The Dry Salvages." Both indicate a failure to see in the particular instance what Eliot's use of language indicates that he saw very clearly in other instances—that no one thing is any other thing; that the experience of God is not a knowledge of Him, nor knowledge experience; that the suffering of the Holy, though it far transcends, does not supplant the science of the Holy or, for that matter, the science of the human—of politics and of history. Old factions do not disappear and should not be asked to disappear until the knowledge and belief on which they are predicated are forgotten; the night of God, being a different wisdom, has no bearing on the matter.

Lapses such as these confuse the poetry of the *Quartets* in some measure, but fortunately they are rare. In spite of them we are justified in concluding that Eliot's achievement as a

Christian poet is remarkable, especially for his time and cir-
cumstances. Though he was an heir to modern secularism and
its philosophical errors, he was able to escape most of the
consequences of those errors, of which the confusion of knowl-
edge and experience is perhaps the most grave. Indeed we
might consider the possibility that authentic mysticism, the
pursuit of the way of contemplation, is the discipline best cal-
culated to redeem the philosophical errors of these times.
Without contradicting the psychological processes involved in
intuition, mysticism places spiritual experience on a proper
footing and keeps it distinct from knowledge. In Eliot's case,
in any event, an understanding that what he had experienced
was not God in the being of physical things but God as charity
in the soul saves his poetry from the flaws of idealism and
scepticism which are the heritage of the nineteenth century,
both in poetry and religion. The understanding of the sacred
subject implicit in Eliot's imagery is superior to that which is
articulated in Newman's prose or in Hopkins's metaphors,
and for that superiority of understanding and of the poetry in
which it issues we, like Eliot, owe a profound debt to St. John
of the Cross. It is clearly the latter who made it possible for
Eliot to possess and take keen delight in the true subject of
Christian art.[18] Because Hopkins had the experience but missed
the meaning, he falls short, in his poetry, of the fullness of that
possession and delight.

Maritain, Gilson, and
Poetic Knowledge

UNFORTUNATELY Eliot's success does not solve the problem of how to write sacred poetry in a secular age—an age that is too profoundly infected with philosophical scepticism to believe in the authenticity of metaphysical or theological wisdom. Any poet may profit from a knowledge of metaphysics and from a belief in its capacity to deal with the mystery of existence; and any Christian poet has access by the virtue of faith to theological wisdom. However, only those men who have a special vocation can enter upon the contemplative way. For that matter it seems likely that a special gift is requisite even to understand what an entrance upon that way means or demands (and one suspects that Eliot's was the latter gift). Unless the person who has been called either to the practice or to the understanding of that way has also the poet's gift, he can scarcely write about the experience of God in the soul. Consequently mystical wisdom is not likely to be the subject of very much poetry in any age, and it can scarcely be recommended as a "solution" to the Christian poet's problem. Indeed to do so would be to profane a rare gift. Eliot is quite right when he says that St. John of the Cross did not write "for you and me," and the way of the *Quartets* is closed to most writers, even to most of those who believe the same doctrines which Eliot believed. It is clear therefore that if we are to recapture "the great song," we must recapture those intellectual modes of vision which gave Dante access in metaphor to a genuine science of invisible things. If we are to have Christian poetry other than the poetry of mystical experience, the truths which are the subjects of that poetry must be made accessible to the speculative intellect and, thereby, to language and metaphor.

Two twentieth-century Thomists, Etienne Gilson and Jacques Maritain, have attempted with remarkable success to recover metaphysics and theology for our time. Indeed a study such as this one is possible only on account of their efforts. They have in effect jumped backward past Newman and the Victorian Catholic revival with its taint of scepticism and subjectivism and sought to close the considerable gap between thirteenth and twentieth-century Catholicism—that gap which Eliot and Tate lament and which has made the writing of Christian poetry in the modern world all but impossible. Both have written extensively on poetry and the other arts, and an examination of their respective literary theories offers itself as a logical and necessary conclusion of this book.[1] On the other hand it may not be precisely the sort of conclusion that a person who had read only their metaphysical, theological, and historical work would expect; unfortunately we cannot bring them forward as the exponents of esthetic theories equal to the requirements of sacred poetry. The latter is what we would expect from them—theoretical justifications of St. Thomas's vision of the world as the legitimate subject matter of poetry. Oddly enough, though both praise Dante and though Gilson wrote a remarkably perceptive book about him, neither is prepared to admit in theory what Dante's poetry contains in fact. On the contrary both insist that the poet must settle for a mode of understanding which seems to be virtually identical with intuition or confused cognition. Both are remarkably modern, sceptical, and subjective in their understanding of poetry, and the discrepancy between those views and their altogether clear perception of Thomist teaching on philosophical and theological matters demands close scrutiny. If we can understand it, we may be able, if not to correct it—which would require another book—at least to suggest the direction in which one might work to correct it. If nothing else we may be able to locate the sources of that discrepancy, and that in itself will be a worthy undertaking. We can scarcely afford to allow

Gilson's and Maritain's twentieth-century views of poetry, products of the very scepticism and subjectivism they have sought to vanquish, to cheat twentieth-century poets of what they won for them by their heroic backward leap.

II

Let us begin with Maritain whose writings on poetry, if not the more profound, have certainly been the more influential of the two. His fundamental thesis in respect to poetry is that the Thomist doctrine of the agent intellect, the active power of the mind which abstracts species from the composite substances which the senses apprehend, can be applied to poetry as well as to metaphysics. The problem which he poses is how to resolve the antinomy between reason and poetic inspiration which exists in philosophy from Plato onward: how "to show that, in spite of all, poetry and the intellect are of the same race and blood, and call to one another"; how "to make the Platonic Muse descend into the soul of man, where she is no longer Muse but creative intuition; and Platonic inspiration descend into the intellect united with imagination, where inspiration from above the soul becomes inspiration from above conceptual reason, that is, poetic experience." His solution depends upon a doctrine of "a spiritual unconscious, or rather, preconscious, of which Plato and the ancient wise men were well aware, and the disregard of which in favor of the Freudian unconscious alone is a sign of the dullness of our times." It is from this "deep nonconscious world of activity, for the intellect and the will . . . [that] the acts and fruits of human consciousness and the clear perceptions of the mind emerge." "Far beneath the sunlit surface thronged with explicit concepts and judgments, words and expressed resolutions or movements of the will, are the sources of knowledge and creativity, of love and suprasensuous desires, hidden in the primordial translucid night of the intimate vitality of the soul" (*Creative Intuition*, pp. 90–91, 94). In this depth—but remember that it is a depth of the intellect, not a subrational, Freudian abyss

—is the activity of the intellect whose operation precedes the conscious world of concepts and syllogisms; and also in this depth is the perceptive power of poetry.

The distinction between these powers is that one is illuminative, the other creative. Each grasps its respective object with an immediacy which is more direct than concepts are capable of; but whereas the grasp of the agent intellect bears fruit in concepts, that of the poetic intuition issues in the images which the poet makes. In other words one is directed toward knowing, the other toward making; but Maritain insists that both are activities of the intellect, and in so far as both are preconscious and in so far as both are ordained to the "things" which the senses perceive, we may regard them as intimately related to one another, powers whose operations are analogous. In fact they are so nearly similar that, as Maritain points out, they have even been the subjects of similar misunderstandings; for just as Plato confused the preconscious and intuitive powers of the poet with the activity of a god or muse, the Arabian philosophers confused the agent intellect with the activity either of God Himself or of some other Intellect distinct from the human. "The myth of the Muse signifies that the source of poetry is separate from the human intellect, outside of it, in the transcendent eternal fatherland of subsisting Ideas. A conception which is akin, in the realm of art, to the Averroistic conception of the separate Intellect in the realm of knowledge" (*Creative Intuition*, p. 87). It is only when we realize that these powers are powers *of the intellect* and that they are closely bound to one another that we can save poetry from the epistemological idealism (and scepticism) which besets both Platonism and Averroism.

At this point in Maritain's discussion we may say, so far, so good; by drawing an analogy between the operations of the Muse and those of the agent intellect he certainly seems to have resolved—or at least to have laid the groundwork for resolving—the antinomy between scientific and poetic knowledge. Indeed one would think that the logical consequence of Maritain's premises would be the justification of metaphysical and theological concept as the legitimate material of poetry. However, the very reverse is the case; for no sooner has he drawn the analogy in question than he proceeds to demonstrate that it is not, in fact, a very close one. Though the agent intellect and the poet's gift of intuition are both capacities of the same human soul, their modes of operation differ as vastly as their respective names would indicate. Whereas the agent intellect abstracts species and produces concepts, the poetic intuition abjures both abstractions and their conceptual fruit. Without abstraction, conceptual cognition is impossible, for the *species impressa* can only be derived from the *res extra animam* by the process of abstraction; and unless that species, which Maritain calls an "intelligible germ," is implanted in the soil of the mind there can be no conceptual fruition. In poetic intuition, since there is no abstraction, the poet somehow grasps the species *in* the individualizing matter of the *res,* in the composite substance. Moreover Maritain makes it very clear that the species which the poet grasps is not the same intelligible species with which the metaphysician deals but rather "another kind of germ, which does not tend toward a concept to be formed." In other words, poetic knowledge is not to be regarded as a union between the intellect and the intelligible form of the thing known but rather as a union which involves, somehow, the substance in its totality. That seems to be what Maritain means when he calls this other kind of germ "an intellective form or act fully determined though enveloped in the night of the spiritual unconscious" (*Creative Intuition,* p. 112). The language is elusive, but one suspects that "an intellective form or act fully determined" is one which is fully involved in the matter which individualizes or "determines" it, inseparable from that matter by abstraction, and for that reason "enveloped in . . . unconsciousness."

That interpretation of Maritain's phrase seems to be borne out by subsequent comments. For instance he speaks of poetic knowledge as "knowledge in act, but nonconceptual knowledge," and it seems clear that knowledge in act implies necessarily a grasp of the composite rather than an abstraction of its form. He appears to be making the same point when he says that such knowledge can be "fully expressed only in the work," for the work presumably conveys the grasp of the substance in the wholeness of its existence. Indeed he goes on to say that the work "plays the part played in ordinary knowledge by the concepts and judgments [acts of *compositio*] produced within the mind." He also calls poetic knowledge "a specific kind of knowledge through . . . affective connaturality which . . . tends to express itself in a work." It is a knowledge which is inseparable from sensible things, not merely at its point of origin but at any stage in its process, and which therefore can only be uttered in the language of the sense, in the work of art. Because it grasps the *res extra animam* by connaturality rather than by abstraction it necessarily expresses that *res* in its composite wholeness rather than in terms of a conceptual definition. In short, "poetic intuition is not directed toward essences, for essences are disengaged from concrete reality in a concept, a universal idea, and scrutinized by means of reasoning; . . . poetic intuition is directed toward concrete existence as connatural to the soul pierced by a given emotion" (*Creative Intuition,* pp. 112, 118, 125–26).

Maritain makes the same point in a different context in *Art and Scholasticism.* There his concern is with the definition of beauty as the "splendor of form," and he remarks that "this brilliance of the form, no matter how purely intelligible it may be in itself, is seized *in the sensible and through the sensible,* and not separately from it." Consequently he asserts that "the intuition of artistic beauty . . . stands at the opposite extreme from the abstraction of scientific truth." That is so because in the intuition of beauty "it is through the very apprehension of the sense that the light of being penetrates the intelligence." In fact, "in the perception of the beautiful" it is the senses which serve to place the intellect "in the presence of a radiant intelligibility (derived, like every intelligibility, in the last analysis from the first intelligibility of the divine Ideas)." Insofar as that "radiant intelligibility" is grasped in terms of its beauty, it "cannot be disengaged or separated from its sense matrix and consequently does not procure an intellectual knowledge expressible in a concept." Therefore if the intellect "turns away from sense to abstract and reason, it turns away from its joy and loses contact with this radiance" (pp. 25–26, 163–64).

III

When we consider Maritain's theory in retrospect, the question which we immediately ask ourselves is whether knowledge conceived as "affective connaturality" and as incapable of conceptual expression is really knowledge at all. If it *is* knowledge by some stretch of the definition, it is certainly not the kind of knowledge which Maritain describes so well in his metaphysical and theological works and upon which Dante based his images. Here then is the discrepancy to which we alluded at the outset between Maritain the Thomist philosopher and Maritain the poetic theorist, for the latter Maritain is clearly offering us a doctrine of cognition that is much closer to "real apprehension" or "instress" than to authentic understanding. If we cannot resolve or correct the discrepancy, can we at least account for its existence, trace it to its sources? I believe we can, for Maritain's logic is very clear.

The problem is simply this: he believes that the poet's subject, the thing which the poem expresses, is not something external to him but rather his own subjectivity. Perhaps Maritain's clearest statement of that belief is the one which we find in his very short and relatively unfamiliar book, *The Situation of Poetry*.[2] There he explains that though the art of poetry presupposes knowledge of some kind, that presupposition is "only the exterior of the mystery." To plumb that mystery we must recognize that the poet's grasp of external things is only preliminary and that those things are not the principal ingredients in the poem. "What is it that an act of thought which in its essence is creative . . . expresses and manifests in producing its work, *if not the very being and substance of him who creates?*"[3]

Upon hearing Maritain say such a thing, the question which immediately comes to mind is why does one need to concern himself at all with the distinction between knowledge and intuition in reference to the *res extra animam?* If poetry is self-expression, why should the poet even bother with things outside himself, much less worry about how he perceives them? The answer is that self-expression, which is the very life of poetry, is impossible unless the self is waked to consciousness by the impinging on it of things external to it. Maritain reminds us that "the substance of a man is obscure to himself; it is in receiving and suffering things, in awaking to the world, that it awakes to itself." Therefore the poet "cannot express his own substance in a work except on the condition that things resound in him, and that within him, in a single awakening, those things and his own substance rise together out of sleep."[4] Hence we see that poetic intuition *is* necessary to the poet's activity, but not in order to grasp the being of things. Rather by grasping those things he is able to apprehend and express himself. Hence, though what is *"most immediate"* among the attainments of poetic intuition "is the experience of the things of the world, . . . what is *most principal* is the experience of the Self" (*Creative Intuition*, pp. 127–28).

It is not difficult to see why this emphasis upon the subjectivity of the poet requires the substitution of intuitive experience for knowledge. Whereas intelligible things—which is to say spiritual things—can be known, material or sensible things cannot; they can only be experienced. Consequently though a man can know his intellect by reflection upon his own acts of cognition, he must rely on intuition for a grasp of those affective faculties "whose soul is sense." Therefore, since a man's subjectivity is a composite of intellectual and affective faculties, the only way he can apprehend his whole being is under the aspect of experience.[5] That is why Maritain describes the poet's "creative intuition [as] . . . an obscure grasping of his own Self and of things in a knowledge through union or through connaturality which is born in the spiritual unconscious, and which fructifies only in the work" (*Creative Intui-*

tion, p. 115; cf. *Situation of Poetry,* p. 51). It is an "obscure grasping . . . born in the spiritual unconscious" because what is grasped includes sense experience which, by its nature, cannot be made lucid or conscious in concept. It is by union or connaturality rather than by abstraction because the self *in its wholeness* (like the thing in its wholeness which the self is grasping) cannot be known by abstractive cognition. (It is no accident that Maritain calls this connaturality "affective"—an "affective connaturality" which wakes the self to a nonconceptual awareness of "the substantial totality of the human person" [*Creative Intuition,* p. 113]). Finally it is an awareness which can only bear fruit in the work, for the work can convey, as the concept cannot, the very experience of the simultaneous apprehension of self and thing and of the awaking which is the immediate consequence. Hence he says that the work "tends finally to convey to the soul of others . . . the same poetic intuition which was in the soul of the poet." Indeed its very purpose is to cause "a communication of intuition, a passage from creative intuition to receptive intuition" (*Creative Intuition,* p. 307).

We see therefore that it is the definition of poetry as discovery and expression of the self which requires Maritain to deny to it the authentic knowledge of the truth of things which he guards so jealously for metaphysics and theology. His reasoning is altogether logical once we grant his original premise. But suppose he is wrong about the whole matter of subjectivity. Suppose, in fact, that the purpose of poetry is to express in an image the truth and beauty of the thing external to the poet's soul—in S. H. Butcher's felicitous phrase, to express "the concrete thing under an image which answers to its true idea."[6] In that case there would be no reason to deny and indeed every reason to affirm that poetic knowledge is not generically or even specifically distinct from philosophical knowledge. To make the latter affirmation would certainly not be tantamount to identifying poetry with theology or metaphysics; but it would serve to locate the difference between the sciences and the art in the poet's mode of expressing his subject rather than in his mode of apprehending it. Were we to approach poetry from the latter point of view, we should place our emphasis on the poet's utterance rather than upon the nature of his cognition or experience.

The latter seems to me the more accurate emphasis because it coincides more nearly than Maritain's with the way in which poets actually deal with their subjects. A Shakespearean tragedy seems to be sufficient evidence that the poet does not necessarily know his subject in terms of an experience of self. The *Comedy*, as we have shown, presents the same kind of evidence and more strikingly perhaps than any other single poem for the simple reason that its subject altogether transcends the reach of intuitive experience or self-awareness. Had Dante been forced to work within the limits of Maritain's thesis, he could not have possessed his subject. That he did take possession of it—and in a masterful fashion—would seem to indicate that his mode of knowing it was not distinct from that of a philosopher or theologian. The difference therefore between the *Comedy* and the *Summa* must lie in Dante's and Aquinas's respective uses of and modes of expressing their common knowledge rather than in epistemological diversity. One is inclined to think that Maritain has mistaken ends for means: seeing that there is a vast difference between poetry and philosophy, he has mistakenly sought the source of that difference in the poet's mode of apprehending his subject rather than in his expression of it. Because the poet unquestionably does express his knowledge *"through the sensible,"* Maritain has concluded incorrectly that he seizes it *"in the sensible."*

IV

In view of the fact that it is Maritain's emphasis on the subjectivity of the poet which causes the discrepancy between his esthetics and his Thomist metaphysics, it is important to remember that the idea (and practice) of poetry as self-expression results from intellectual circumstances which are radically opposed to Thomism. In fact it is a product of that very scepticism which Maritain resists so persuasively in his interpretation of St. Thomas's epistemology.

Perhaps the best way to demonstrate that fact is to listen to the comments of a contemporary critic whose own bias is modern and sceptical, who seems to prefer "poetry of experience" to poetry of Dante's sort, but who sees very clearly that the differences between the two are to be traced to the divergent philosophical assumptions which give rise to them. I refer to Robert Langbaum, who has defined with great clarity the difference between "the modern symbol" (or the "Wordsworthian object") and "the symbols of Dante or Spenser": "In the allegorical poetry of the Middle Ages and Renaissance, the symbol stands in a one-to-one relation for an external idea or system of ideas." In other words, in medieval and renaissance poetry the symbol expresses something known independently of the poem or of the poet's perception—"an *external* idea or system of ideas." Therefore it is legitimate to regard the symbol as a means of expressing something known or understood rather than as the communication of an experience. "But the modern symbol exists as an object for imaginative penetration. Although any number of ideas may be applied to it as problematical interpretations, its ultimate meaning is itself, its own 'life,' which is to say the observer's life inside it."[7]

We recognize immediately that the "observer's life inside" the symbol is precisely what Maritain is talking about when he treats poetry as a mode of self-expression. The symbol ceases to represent the idea of the *res extra animam* because the "most principal" concern of the poem is to convey "the experience of the Self." Its "inner life" (the symbol's or the poem's, the part's or the whole's) is the poet's life, and external things are important principally in terms of that life. Hopkins, as we might have expected, serves Langbaum as a good illustration of his thesis: "Hopkins meant [by inscape] the individuality or *thisness* as opposed to the categorical *whatness* of a thing, its *selfness* as perceived through 'That taste of myself, of *I* and *me* above and in all things.'" Hopkins, like Mallarmé and like Wordsworth, "wanted to get beneath categorical meaning to the object itself," which is simply to say that he wanted to substitute an experience of the thing for a knowledge of it. In order to do that he sought "that point in perception where the object is perceived from inside because perceived together with the self in one concrete experience."[8]

The last phrase offers itself as a very exact summary of Maritain's theory of poetic perception—the fusion into a single experience of the grasp of the self and of the external thing. However, Langbaum perceives, as Maritain ironically does not, that a Thomist has no business expounding such a theory. The modern symbol, which Langbaum also calls an "epiphany" and which he characterizes as "the essential innovation of *Lyrical Ballads,*" is "a way of apprehending value when value is no longer objective—when it is no longer in nature, which is to say in a publicly accepted order of ideas about nature." If we may adapt Langbaum's statement to the language of this study, we should say that the modern symbol is "a way of apprehending value" when men lose confidence in the capacity of the intellect to discern the essences and the order of the essences—much less the presence of God "innermostly" as their source of existence. The retreat from *whatness* to *thisness* is a consequence of scepticism, of doubt that the intellect can abstract the form and know the quiddity of the things which the senses perceive—indeed of doubt that the things of the physical world are intelligible. In such a view of the creation the only possible value that the *res extra animam* can have is that which is given it in the poet's experience of it. Hence he "grounds the statement of value in perception," and by doing so he "gives us the idea . . . before we have to pass judgment on its truth or falsity, before it has been abstracted from perception—while it is still in union with emotion and the perceived object."[9]

In this new kind of symbol, says Langbaum, "we can discern a distinctively modern form of literature"—a form, that is, which takes its rise from conditions of philosophical scepticism and religious doubt. Though an orthodox Catholic like

Hopkins may write in this form, to the extent that he does so "he is, in spite of his Catholic orthodoxy, a 'modern' poet."[10] The phrase "in spite of" gives Langbaum's theory precisely the perspective which Maritain's lacks. The latter has attempted to build upon the metaphysical and epistemological premises of Catholic orthodoxy a thoroughly modern theory of poetry without, it seems, taking full account of the consequences. At least he does not appear to have recognized that an esthetic theory built on subjective experience does little if any justice to the finest poetry of our civilization, most of which was written on radically different assumptions and in intellectual circumstances much closer to St. Thomas's than to Newman's and Hopkins's. That fact alone seems sufficient reason for questioning Maritain's distinction between poetic intuition and metaphysical or theological knowledge. The poet's mode of perception may indeed be distinct from the metaphysician's or theologian's, but one wonders if the distinction is precisely what Maritain conceives it to be. Does the poet in fact grasp another kind of "intellectual germ" from the *species impressa* which seeds conceptual cognition? Or is it possible that the uniqueness of the Muse's activity is to be found, not in epistemology, but in art—not in the way a poet knows but in the way he puts his knowledge to use in a poem? All of these are questions which would have to be considered by anyone who might someday undertake to revise or correct Maritain's work. For the moment we need only pose them and suggest that they point to the obstacle which hinders his application of genuinely Thomist insights to poetry.

V

Gilson's approach to poetry is radically different from Maritain's. Gilson does in fact what we have suggested that Maritain should have done—he focuses his attention upon the work of art rather than upon the mode of cognition which precedes it. Indeed he devotes a lengthy footnote to the difference between his approach and Maritain's (*Painting and Reality*,

p. 4, n. 1). We might therefore expect him to be less suscepti-
ble than Maritain to modern, subjective theories of cognition
and less prone to a discrepancy between metaphysical and
esthetic insights. What happens, however, is that his emphasis
upon the work of art as an existing reality in its own right
leads to his insistence that it is not to convey or communicate
or express or represent anything; it is simply to be. Like all
works of art the poem is to be regarded as a substance, or at
least what we might call a "quasi-substance," composite of
form and matter, whose chief justification is not to mean but
to exist. That, we recognize at once, is also a modern theory of
the nature of poetry, closely kin to the theory of poetry as ex-
perience and, historically speaking, a product of similar intel-
lectual circumstances. We are therefore not surprised that the
pursuit of it leads Gilson far afield from his fundamental
Thomism and to conclusions virtually identical with Maritain's.

Since the form is the vital principle of any substance, we
may best understand Gilson's thesis in terms of what he con-
ceives the form of a work of art to be. If I understand him cor-
rectly, form in art is primarily shape or order—"that arrange-
ment which makes the parts of a whole out of a plurality of
elements and thereby structures the latter into a distinct ob-
ject." Indeed "we speak of a being only when we can grasp a
plurality in a principle of unity which is precisely its form."
Thus in the work of art as in the natural substance the "scho-
lastic adage" holds true, that *"forma dat esse."* The principle is
borne out in practical experience, for "to say that a symphony,
a poem or any book is 'formless' is tantamount to denying its
existence" (*Forms and Substances,* p. 4). Gilson lays heavy
stress upon this fundamental premise, that "among the proper-
ties of form, the most striking one is its aptitude to confer be-
ing upon the matter that receives it." That aptitude, he insists,
is not merely a deduction from theology or metaphysics ap-
plied to the work of art. In fact just the reverse is true, for
"when theologians started from the visible world in order to
conceive, as best they could, the invisible nature of God, they
first borrowed from art the pattern of the most perfect kind of

causality given in human experience, and then transcended it in order to make it attributable to God." The principle, in short, is drawn from the empirical observation that artists give being to a work by imposing form on matter. It is simply impossible to isolate the power to give existence from the power to shape, define, or delineate, and Gilson mentions the "passionate interest we all experience in watching the tip of a painting brush or a pencil while it actually delineates objects, or men and women, that seem to spring from nothingness [by virtue of that delineation] before our very eyes" (*Painting and Reality,* pp. 121, 124, 126).

From these remarks on the capacity of form to give existence to a work of art Gilson proceeds to the principal tenet of his thesis: that the artist's purpose is not to express something but rather to make a beautiful object—a house, a statue, a painting, a string quartet, or a poem. In fact Gilson begins *The Arts of the Beautiful* with a very clear statement to that effect: "In the *Encyclopédie française* we find this quotation by the historian Lucien Febvre: 'Assuredly, art is a kind of knowledge.' The present book rests upon the firm and considered conviction that art is *not* a kind of knowledge or, in other words, that it is not a manner of knowing." (p. 9). Rather it is a manner of making, of bringing into existence objects of various sorts which previously had no existence. In fact Gilson does not flinch before the word *create*—the artist is not a knower but, by virtue of his ability to impose form on matter, a creator. Gilson is careful to hedge this doctrine around with all sorts of cautions, for he does not want anyone to confuse the creative artist with God or to ascribe to the former the proper operation of the latter. He reminds us for instance that both the artist who imposes form, the form which he imposes, and the matter on which he imposes it have been created by God; that the artist and everything with which he deals "are enjoying an actual existence they have received from the Prime Cause" (*Painting and Reality,* p. 120). Therefore the artist should never flatter himself that he creates in an absolute sense; however, the fact remains that within the limits of his own contingency and the contingency of the things with which he works, the artist can communicate existence to the object he makes. That communication, that making, is his justification.

Gilson is nothing if not fair in the application of his thesis, and he is perfectly willing to admit that the classical definition of art as imitation (and consequently as a mode of knowing and expressing) has venerable precedent. For one thing he is too good an Aristotelian to ignore mimesis altogether. For another, his reminder that the artist does not create in an absolute sense entails as its corollary the reminder that he cannot make without, in some manner, copying what God has made. Consider for instance contemporary, nonrepresentational statuary, which does not intend to imitate or signify anything in nature. On the one hand the very fact that such work exists proves Gilson's thesis: the artist's object is to give existence by imposing form upon matter. The nonrepresentational statue fulfills that requirement without signifying anything. It has achieved a "formal beauty in its pure state"—the beauty that derives simply from its existence. However, having established that point, Gilson is quick to admit that such pure sculpture has not, in fact, produced the great statuary art of our civilization, and he adds that the traditional "basis of statuary in imitation is a salutary warning against overdoing the systematization of philosophical reflections on the fine arts." Moreover, though nonrepresentational sculpture sets itself the "aim of obtaining a purely formal beauty free of any imitation of natural objects of any kind, save that of the ineluctable necessity of being an object," that very necessity binds the work, however tenuously, to mimesis: "making a 'thing' is still an imitation of reality" (*Forms and Substances,* pp. 88, 96, 97).

These qualifications of Gilson's thesis are closely linked to his discussion of the second component of the artistic substance, the matter on which the artist works. Though form gives being, the matter to which it gives that being has a great deal to say about what the composite will be. Indeed the role of matter in art is more important than in nature, for whereas

the natural form is imposed on "prime matter," which is pure
potentiality and which does not exist until it is formed, the
artist works with matter which is an existing substance pos-
essing a natural form before the artistic form is imposed upon
it. Indeed we might say that the artist's matter is more like
signate matter, which gives individuality, than like prime
matter. That is an inexact analogy, but in one respect at least
it holds true: the matter in each case exerts a determining in-
fluence upon the form. "Stone, wood, color, musical sound or
a written or spoken word . . . are called materials, despite
their forms, because the artist freely takes possession of them
in order to make works of art out of them." However, because
"this matter is . . . some substance already determined by its
form, the artist using it as a material is forced to take account
of its natural formal determinations in the artistic use that he
makes of it." He is free, as Gilson notes, to choose the material
with which he will work, "but once his decision has been made
his art must respect the conditions imposed by the natural
form of the material on which he will have chosen to exer-
cise his skill" (*Forms and Substances*, p. 29). The grain in the
marble will exert a determining influence upon the statue; the
kind of paint and color on the painting.

Hence Gilson speaks of the "vocation" of matter, drawing
from Focillon's *The Life of Forms in Art* the principle that
" 'all different kinds of matter are subject to a certain destiny,
or at all events, to a certain formal vocation' " (*Forms and
Substances*, p. 5). He embellishes that principle with reference
to Aristotle's famous formula " 'that what desires the form is
matter, as the female desires the male and the ugly the beauti-
ful' " (*Painting and Reality*, p. 109).[11] We might say that any
given matter beckons to itself the form which is proper to it.
Therefore, says Gilson, "when the sculptor asks himself whether
a block of marble shall be a god, a table or a basin, the marble
has something to say about it. In its own way, in fact, it is the
first to speak, announcing its vocation." That announcement
establishes "an intelligible relation between material form and
artistic form; the form that art imparts to matter does not

come to it exclusively from without." Rather "matter aspires to the form potential in it" (*Forms and Substances,* pp. 30, 79).

VI

The last statement brings us face to face with an inconsistency in Gilson's artistic theory which is analogous to the larger inconsistency or discrepancy between his artistic theory and his Thomist theology and metaphysics. If we take his conception of the artist as creator to its logical conclusion, we must finally say, as Gilson does, that a poem cannot convey knowledge— that it must simply exist and that its justification is to be a beautiful object. If on the other hand we pursue the idea that "matter aspires to the form potential in it," remembering as we do so that words are the matter of poetry, we are driven to the conclusion that the poem, by virtue of its matter, *must* have knowledge as its object. What, after all, is the form potential in verbal matter if not the meaning of the words? If Gilson had pursued the latter view rather than the former, if he had taken the theory of matter's vocation to its logical conclusion, he would almost certainly have produced a theory of poetry congruent with his theology and metaphysics and equal to the demands of sacred poetry; for once we grant that the meaning of words is the primary aspect of their vocation as matter, we are constrained to say that philosophical and theological concepts may become part of the poem's substance. We are therefore disposed to believe that any effort to correct Gilson's thesis must begin with a consideration of words as matter in artistic substance.

The best way to do that is to see what Gilson himself says on the subject, and what we find in fact is that his statements are inconsistent. That inconsistency, however, is not surprising, for the very nature of words works at cross purposes with his primary thesis that the poem is only to be. He admits for instance that "poetry finds itself in a particular situation [with reference to the other arts], owing to the fact that its material is language." Because "a word signifying nothing would not be a word," and because the "essence of poetry [is] to be fashioned out of words as its proper material, an element of signification necessarily enters into the composition of any poetry." On the other hand, "it does not follow that poetry's object is to signify anything whatever: concepts, images or feelings." At first glance the two statements seem to contradict one another. The only thing that saves the logic of the argument is the word *object*. Gilson is saying that poetry, by virtue of its verbal matter, does necessarily convey knowledge, but to do so is not its aim. In other words poetry cannot help signifying, but it is not "authorized to do so except to the degree that it can do this without making it impossible for it to achieve its proper end which is to create beauty with words" (*Forms and Substances,* pp. 223, 225). That is not, strictly speaking, an illogical statement, but it does lead to the paradoxical conclusion that poetry's matter is a liability to the art.

Gilson is forced into some rather circuitous arguments in an ultimately unsuccessful attempt to resolve that paradox. He must explain how poetry can "create beauty with words," whose purpose is signification, without having signification for its object. In my own estimation he does not make a satisfactory job of the explanation; rather he evades, in the last analysis, the fact that words mean. His argument is constructed on the proposition that the poet uses words, not with regard to their meaning, but to what he calls their "harmonics." "Verbal structure . . . is not dictated . . . by the rules of logic, no matter how flexible one might make them." Instead words are so employed that each "strikes home and resonances of all kinds radiate into the mind from around its point of impact." It is the interrelationships among those various resonances, rather than their intelligible relationships, which determine the use of the word in the poem. Nor is it possible "to foresee which of these harmonics will go to seek, among those of another word, the elected one which will let this very word spring up along with the whole retinue of its different resonances." Gilson does not deny that "the conceptual meaning of the word is included in its harmonics," and we may conclude therefore that its signification is one constituent of its resonance; however, that is as much of meaning as he seems willing to allow us (*Forms and Substances*, pp. 214–15). Consequently we are not surprised to hear him conclude in language very close to Maritain's that "artistic beauty partakes of the intelligible," not directly, as the metaphysician's concept does, but rather as the intelligible is "perceived in sensible experience"; or that beauty in art is never abstract and conceptual but "is linked to the material in the object and to the body in the percipient" (*Forms and Substances*, p. 225), a doctrine which, though it has a different source, resembles very closely Maritain's "affective connaturality." Nevertheless the gnawing question persists: how can words, which mean, be used without regard to their meaning? How indeed can they be used for the sake of beauty if their very nature, their formal determination, is ignored? If they do carry meaning, we cannot avoid the conclusion that a sequence or structure composed of them has to be built on their intelligible relations with one another. To deny the latter fact is to contradict the former, and to hold both positions at once (which is what Gilson tries to do) is to equivocate. In any event it does not seem to have occurred to him that the beautiful work which we call a poem is beautiful primarily in terms of its meaning.[12]

To say as much is not to deny that the relationship between words in a poem is vastly different from what we find in prose but rather to suggest that the difference is not at the expense of "their intelligible meaning . . . which is their truth" (*Forms and Substances*, p. 225). Gilson's metaphor of resonance is in fact a very good one, for words in a poem are linked together by a web of associations which are very much like radiating resonances. On the other hand we find in most poems that their meaning, their truth, is the primary factor in their harmonic pattern and that the echoing and overlapping of sound or "color" or emotional effect is subsidiary to the interlocking of meanings. Consider an exchange between Duncan and Banquo, the richness of which Gilson badly underestimates simply because he does not take meaning into sufficient account:

DUNCAN. This castle hath a pleasant seat; the air
  Nimbly and sweetly recommends itself
  Unto our gentle senses.
BANQUO.   This guest of summer,
  The temple-haunting martlet, does approve,
  By his loved mansionry, that the heaven's breath
  Smells wooingly here: no jutty, frieze,
  Buttress, nor coign of vantage, but this bird
  Hath made his pendent bed and procreant cradle;
  Where they most breed and haunt, I have observed
  The air is delicate.   (*Macbeth*, I, vi)

Gilson's comment on this exceedingly rich passage shows very clearly the limitation which he imposes on poetry by insisting on harmonics to the virtual exclusion of meaning. He remarks that "if what Banquo *says* were the important thing, to say it that way would be ridiculous." He proceeds to translate the exchange into prose:

DUNCAN. My, the air smells good.
BANQUO. Usually, the air is good where swallows make
  their nests, and look, they are nesting all over the place.

Gilson's conclusion is that it is obviously not what Banquo *says* which is important but rather what the poem *is*. "Shakespeare's verbal fireworks are there for their own sake; their very gratuity transfigures the prose element . . . and clothes it in poetic garb" (*Arts of the Beautiful*, p. 65).

 Are these rich verbal intricacies no more than "fireworks"? Are they, with respect to the "prose element," merely gratuitous? The evidence of the play itself seems to contradict that judgment, for the harmonic interrelationship among words in *Macbeth* is very rich in meaning. In fact we might say that the whole significance of the play is captured here in small compass, for, from the first scene to the last, evil is associated with images of cold, of foul, choking air, of sexual sterility, and of unnatural relations among men and things. Goodness, on the contrary, is linked with images of bright, sweet air, of fertility, of natural order, and finally—with specific reference to Edward of England—to holiness. Therefore we see that a "temple-haunting martlet," who builds a "pendent bed, and procreant cradle," who both "breeds" and "haunts' in the sweet air, serves as a kind of composite symbol for one of the poles of the play's meaning. In the allusion to the bird Shakespeare ties together the various attributes of goodness, both physical and spiritual, which define by contrast the significance of Macbeth's tragic choice.

Here indeed are words which strike home and from which "resonances of all kinds radiate into the mind from around [their] point of impact." We never forget the martlet while we are in the world of the play. When Lady Macbeth pleads to the demons to "unsex" her, to take from her breasts her "milk for gall" (I, v), or when she says that she would take "the babe that milks me" (I, vii) and dash out its brains, we think in a sort of spontaneous reflex of the bird's "loved mansionry" and "procreant cradle." Likewise when Shakespeare evokes a picture of holy Edward, who by his solicitation of heaven heals those who are "swoln and ulcerous," who leaves to his successors (a suggestion of natural fertility) "the healing benediction," and about whose throne hang "sundry blessings" which "speak him full of grace" (IV, iii), we recall Banquo's association between the bird's natural goodness and the haunting of temples or "heaven's breath." We could go on with such allusions at great length, for the thematic associations, caught in the imagery of the play, ramify with an exceptional richness. The point, however, should be clear without further illustration: that "what Banquo *says* [is] the important thing," and that that fact is in no way a contradiction of the importance of what the play *is*. The resonances which give the play its unity (and hence its formal existence) carry all kinds of emotional and aural associations, but those are inseparable from, ultimately dependent upon, the meanings of the words which resonate and their intelligible relations with one another.

Moreover it is interesting to note that in *Macbeth* those intelligible relations bring before us a vision of the world which we could legitimately describe as metaphysical and theological. Beneath all the references to fertility and sterility lies Shakespeare's allusion to "nature's germens" which Macbeth invites the witches to "tumble all together, / Even till destruction sicken" (IV, i). Those seeds of nature, *rationes seminales,* originally of Platonic origin, are the sources of her life and order, her sweetness and her fertility. When they are tumbled by demonic powers, all fertility and richness is corrupted. The drama depends in no inconsiderable measure on our understanding that metaphysical fact; it links the activities of the witches with the whole symbolic structure of the play, and it enables us to understand Macbeth's destruction in its full spiritual context.[13] Therefore it does not seem an exaggeration to say that *Macbeth* does *mean* on a very abstract level and that that meaning is the very life of the work.

Indeed we see in *Macbeth* what we have seen in the *Comedy* on a much vaster scale: a poem whose very unity—and consequently whose existence as a work of art—consists in words which carry the weight of philosophical and doctrinal truth. Such poems are alive at every moment with the meaning of the whole: we cannot touch a single image or, in some instances, a single word without touching off reverberations (resonances) throughout the work, and beyond it. That very fact is sufficient testimony to Gilson's central thesis that the work of art is an actually existing substance, having its own life which consists in its formal unity; every part has its significance in terms of the whole. On the other hand that same fact proves that the unity and life of the substance is that of the meaning of its words. It is, I suspect, that fundamental truth about poetry which leads C. S. Lewis to remark that "the greatest prose and poetry are least unlike each other, and that Dante has proved it. When he is most poetical he says most precisely what he really means in the prose sense of the verb to *mean.*"[14] If that statement is a paradox, it is a serious one; and when all is said and done it is perhaps only in the language of paradox—which is the language of mystery—that we can do justice to an art whose existence is its meaning and whose meaning its existence.

VII

Pointing out Gilson's inconsistencies scarcely constitutes a correction of his thesis. These criticisms, like those of Maritain's subjectivism, can do little more than suggest a direction for future study. In fact, of the two, Gilson's work presents the tougher problem, for the debate between meaning and being is older and more complex than that between subjectivity and objectivity. The latter, as an esthetic problem, is peculiar to the modern world. The former goes all the way back to Plato and Aristotle, and the frequency of its manifestation in contemporary criticism is clear indication that it has not yet been resolved. On the other hand it is fair to say that in modern poetry and theory the emphasis on the poet as creator has been disproportionate. Moreover the source of that disproportion is almost certainly the same scepticism which induces Maritain to identify poetic knowledge with intuition. Therefore we may reasonably suggest that just as a revision of Maritain's thesis must begin by disengaging his Thomist epistemology from the modernist notion of subjective experience, so in Gilson's case a correction must take much fuller account than he does of the capacity of words to convey conceptual truth.

How that capacity can be reconciled with the formal demands of art is a further problem; it is probably the fundamental problem with which Gilson's disciples must deal if they are to reconcile his thesis with the facts of poetic composition. The analogous problem for the future students of Maritain is to show how a truth which is seized in abstraction from the things of sense can be expressed by the poet, with no diminution of its conceptual clarity, *in* the things of sense. These are problems which Christian poetry raises in a particularly striking way, for in respect of the issue of poetic knowledge it is the proverbial exception that proves the rule. It is the one kind of poetry which on account of its purely intelligible subject matter—the holy and invisible and unimaginable Godhead—absolutely has to mean in order to be. Since (unless the poet is also a mystic) its subject matter can only be attained by knowledge, it must take conceptual cognitions for its matter if it is to have a matter at all.

The question of the relationship between meaning and existence in poetry is an authentically philosophical one. It centers upon the epistemological relationship between the metaphysician's concept and the poet's image. What, for instance, is the difference between the third act of intellection, the *compositio,* which reunites the abstracted essence with the existing substance, and the activity by which a poet forms an image that presents the substance in respect of its essence? Does the image merely articulate the *compositio?* Does it merely serve as a device for conveying the metaphysician's judgment, or is it the fruit of an analogous intellectual process which is the poet's special gift? That, I believe, is a philosophical as opposed to a critical or technical question, for though we can show how a poet uses language and constructs metaphors in order to express "the concrete thing under an image which answers to its true idea," we must investigate the very life of the intellect and imagination in order to discern the spiritual activity behind the technique. We must seek out that remarkably mysterious point of intersection in the soul where knowing and making unite—where meaning, without ceasing to mean, is translated into artistic being, where the thing known, without ceasing to be the subject of authentic knowledge, becomes a constituent of the thing made, and where the concept, with no loss of its abstract identity, transforms itself into an image accessible to the sense.

The search will clearly not be easy. It may be that that mysterious point of union is too mysterious ever to be discerned. We may have simply to content ourselves with knowing that it exists; but that knowledge, at least, we must adhere to. Neither Maritain nor Gilson does adhere to it, and in the final analysis that is the rock on which both break. Neither faces up to the fact—evident in *Macbeth,* evident in the *Comedy,* evident in fact in most great poetry before the nineteenth century and in some since—that meaning and being, concept and sense image, can and do unite, and unite in such a way as to preserve pure meaning, pure conceptual knowledge, in the very flesh of the sensible artifact. Both evade the mystery of poetry—Gilson by failing to take the meaning of poetic language seriously and Maritain by insisting that poetic knowledge is never conceptual at any stage but rather a knowledge by "affective connaturality." Each, as a consequence of his evasion, deprives himself of a proper understanding of the art with which he deals. Gilson for instance is compelled to argue that in the *Comedy* neither the "universal history . . . nor the philosophy, nor the theology . . . each of which has its characteristic beauty," can be classified as portions of the poetry. Rather, he says, the *Comedy*'s "poetic beauty is attributable to another thing, to that element of pure poetry which flows and circulates throughout this grandiose epic" (*Forms and Substances,* pp. 242–43).[15] What he cannot recognize is that the history, philosophy, and theology, which his own Thomist teachings justify as authentic modes of knowledge, become, by some mysterious alchemy which at once transforms and preserves, the very poetic beauty which flows and circulates through the epic.

We cannot say how, but neither can we gainsay the fact that somehow such a thing does happen. The poem itself is the proof that it happens, and it is the poem with which all speculation must begin and end. We shall never be able to explain how Dante's conceptual subject matter becomes sensible imagery unless we admit that it does. Moreover, unless we confront that fact squarely, we shall have no hope of recovering the conditions necessary for "the great song." Our only delight will be those rattling pebbles whose possession and articulation in image does not entail knowledge and of which we are under no constraint to speak metaphysical and theological truths. Maritain and Gilson have taught us how to speak those truths in St. Thomas's language and have thus made available to us what our Victorian forebears lacked—a conviction that knowledge of the invisible things of God is possible. If we could now proceed to show how their theories of poetry could be made to conform to their own best insights into the nature of truth, we might be able to gain for poetry their potentially inestimable contribution to that art. Moreover, the philosophical premise for such an undertaking might prove to be the very Scholastic definition on which both rely: that art is a virtue of the practical intellect, *recta ratio factibilium.* If we could isolate that definition from Maritain's theory of poetic intuition and from Gilson's preoccupation with existence at the expense of meaning, we might be able to develop a poetics which would be adequate to account for such a work as Dante's. That, however, is a task for other scholars and other books.

Notes

Introduction

1. T. S. Eliot, "Dante," *Selected Essays* (New York: Harcourt, Brace, 1950), p. 219.

2. Allen Tate, "The Symbolic Imagination," *Essays of Four Decades* (Chicago: Swallow, 1968), pp. 429–430.

3. Perhaps the clearest account of St. Thomas's place in the history of Christian theology is to be found in Etienne Gilson, *History of Christian Philosophy in the Middle Ages* (London: Sheed & Ward, 1955).

4. Christopher Dawson, "Newman and the Modern World," *The Tablet,* 5 August 1972, p. 733.

5. *Ibid.*

6. Jacques Maritain, *The Degrees of Knowledge,* trans. Gerald B. Phelan (London: Geoffrey Bles, 1959), pp. 247–253.

7. St. Thomas Aquinas, *Summa Theologica,* II (2), 1, 2. Hereafter cited in the text as *ST.* All references to the *Summa* are to the translation by the Fathers of the English Dominican Province (London: Burns, Oates & Washbourne, 1920–1925), 22 vols.

8. Maritain, *Degrees of Knowledge,* p. 253.

Chapter 1

1. See, for instance, C. S. Lewis, *The Discarded Image* (Cambridge: Cambridge University Press, 1964).

2. Dante Alighieri, *The Divine Comedy,* trans. John D. Sinclair (New York: Oxford University Press, 1948). *Inf.,* i, 7; all citations of the *Comedy* refer to this edition. Sinclair's is

"the critical text of the *Società Dantesca Italiana* as revised by the late Professor Giuseppe Vandelli" (*Inferno*, p. 9).

3. *La Divina Commedia,* ed. C. H. Grandgent (Cambridge: Harvard University Press, 1972), p. 655 (n. 79).

Chapter 2

1. *The Christian Philosophy of St. Thomas Aquinas,* trans. L. K. Shook (London: Victor Gollancz, 1961), p. 225.

2. *Ibid.,* p. 226.

3. *Ibid.,* p. 227.

4. *Ibid.*

5. St. Thomas Aquinas, *Summa Contra Gentiles,* I, 53. Hereafter cited in the text as *CG.* All references to the *Summa Contra Gentiles* are to the translation by Anton C. Pegis et al (Garden City, N. Y.: Doubleday, 1955–1957), 5 vols.

6. *Aquinas,* p. 229.

7. *Ibid.,* pp. 230, 476 (n. 17).

8. *Ibid.,* p. 101.

9. John Henry Newman, *An Essay in Aid of a Grammar of Assent,* ed. Charles Frederick Harrold (London: Longmans, Green, 1947), p. 17. Hereafter cited in the text as *Grammar.*

10. *The Idea of a University* (London: Longmans, Green, 1910), pp. 46, 47, 51.

11. *Apologia Pro Vita Sua,* ed. Martin J. Svaglic (Oxford: Clarendon Press, 1967), pp. 216–17. Hereafter cited in the text as *Ap.*

12. "Proof of Theism," *The Philosophical Notebook of John Henry Newman,* ed. Edward Sillem (Louvain: Nauwelaerts, 1970), II, 31–33. Hereafter cited in the text as *Notebook.*

13. *The Unity of Philosophical Experience* (London: Sheed & Ward, 1955), p. 238.

14. See Eric Przywara, "St. Augustine and the Modern World," in *Saint Augustine* (Cleveland and New York: World, 1964), pp. 249–86.

Chapter 3

1. *Fifteen Sermons Preached Before the University of Oxford* (London: Longmans, Green, 1909), p. 179. Hereafter cited in the text as *Sermons*.

2. See, for instance, Oxford Sermon 13 and in the *Grammar of Assent* Chapter 9, "The Illative Sense," pp. 261–91.

3. *Lectures on the Doctrine of Justification* (London: Longmans, Green, 1908), p. 267. Italics added.

4. *Ibid.*, p. 272.

5. *Aquinas*, p. 13.

Chapter 4

1. The record of the personal acquaintance is to be found in the correspondence. See *Further Letters of Gerard Manley Hopkins*, ed. Claude Colleer Abbot (London: Oxford University Press, 1956), pp. 21–22, 29–30, 63–64, 404–14. It is clear from other correspondence that Hopkins had read the *Difficulties of Anglicans* (see *Further Letters*, p. 51) and that he heard the *Letter to the Duke of Norfolk* read in recreation. (See *The Journals and Papers of Gerard Manley Hopkins*, ed. Humphry House and Graham Storey [London: Oxford University Press, 1959], p. 262. See also *Further Letters*, p. 410.) There is strong evidence but no proof that he read the *Apologia;* his poem "The Half-Way House," written in 1865, the year after the first edition of the *Apologia*, probably echoes Newman's use of the phrase to describe the Anglican Church. See *Ap.*, p. 185. For Hopkins's interest in the *Grammar of Assent* see pp. 76–77.

2. "Tintern Abbey," 1. 49.

3. See, for instance, Etienne Gilson, *Reason and Revelation in the Middle Ages* (New York: Scribner's, 1952), pp. 8 ff.

4. In this matter we must distinguish between theory and fact. In theory the position of the Church of Rome has not altered.

5. For Hopkins's discovery of Scotus see *Journals and Papers,* p. 221. For his discovery of the *Grammar of Assent* see *Further Letters,* p. 58.

6. *Further Letters,* p. 412.

7. *The Sermons and Devotional Writings of Gerard Manley Hopkins,* ed. Christopher Devlin (London: Oxford University Press, 1959), p. 312. Hereafter cited in the text as *SD*.

8. Father Devlin makes the interesting observation that Hopkins would naturally have been attracted to Scotus's epistemological ideas in 1872, "for he had 'done' epistemology in the first year of his course of philosophy (1870–1), and was now engaged upon psychology." See Christopher Devlin, "The Image and the Word," *The Month,* n.s. 3 (1950): 114–27; 191–202. Passage quoted is on p. 114.

9. *Duns Scotus: The Basic Principles of His Philosophy,* trans. Bernardine Bonansea (Washington: Catholic University of America Press, 1961), pp. 20, 21.

10. *Jean Duns Scot* (Paris: Librairie Philosophique J. Vrin, 1952), pp. 518–19.

11. Ioannis Duns Scoti, *Opera Omnia,* ed. P. Carolo Balić (Civitas Vaticana: Typis Polyglottis Vaticanis, 1950–   ), III, 267. (*Opus Oxoniense,* I, d.3, p. 3, qu.2, n. 11). Hereafter cited as Scotus.

12. For a clear statement of the difference between the Scholastic and modern ideas of intuition see the OED entry. For the distinction in specific reference to Scotus see Sebastian J. Day, *Intuitive Cognition* (St. Bonaventure, N. Y.: Franciscan Institute, 1947). Hereafter cited as Day.

13. Quoted by Day, p. 72, from *Opus Oxoniense,* II, d.3, qu.9, n. 6.

14. Scotus II, 23 (*Opus Oxoniense,* I, d.1, p.1, qu.2, n. 3).

15. Quoted by Day, p. 72, from *Opus Oxoniense,* II, d.3, qu.9, n. 6.

16. *Aquinas,* p. 42.

17. Scotus, p. 73. Scotus makes the distinction between names and definitions quite clear in the *Opus Oxoniense,* I, d.3, p. 1, qu.1–2, n. 21 (Scotus, III, 50): *Sed confuse aliquid*

dicitur concipi quando concipitur sicut exprimitur per nomen,
—distincte, quando concipitur sicut exprimitur per definitio-
nem.

18. "Hopkins and Duns Scotus," *New Verse,* no. 14, April,
1935, p. 13. Hereafter cited as *NV.*

19. Scotus, III, 50, n. A. (*Opus Oxoniense,* I, d.3, p. 1,
qu.1–2, n. 22).

20. *Ibid.,* 234 (*Opus Oxoniense,* I, d.3, p. 3, qu.1, n. 17).

21. *Jean Duns Scot,* p. 74.

22. Besides the articles on Hopkins and Scotus by Devlin
mentioned elsewhere, see his "Time's Eunuch," *The Month,*
n.s. 1 (1949): 303–12. See also W. H. Gardner, "A Note on
Hopkins and Duns Scotus," *Scrutiny,* 5 (1936): 61–70;
Marjorie D. Coogan, "Inscape and Instress: Further Analogies
with Scotus," *PMLA,* 65 (1950): 66–74.

23. "An Essay on Scotus," *The Month,* 182 (1946): 460.

24. We must not forget that Newman allows for a notional
theology in very much the same spirit that one allows for a
necessary evil.

25. *NV,* p. 13.

26. *Ibid.,* pp. 13–14.

27. Quoted by Devlin in *SD,* p. 296, from *Quaestiones
Reportatae Parisienses,* III, vii, 4.

28. See Devlin's explanation of Hopkins's distinction be-
tween *Ensarkosis* and *Enanthropesis, SD,* p. 114.

29. All citations of Hopkins's poems refer to *The Poems of
Gerard Manley Hopkins,* 4th edition, ed. W. H. Gardner and
N. H. Mackenzie (London: Oxford University Press, 1967).

30. Miller, *The Disappearance of God* (New York:
Schocken, 1965), p. 315. Pick, *Gerard Manley Hopkins, Priest
and Poet* (New York: Oxford University Press, 1966), pp.
56–57. Gardner, *Gerard Manley Hopkins* (London: Oxford
University Press, 1966), II, 234–35. Schneider, *The Dragon in
the Gate* (Berkeley: University of California Press, 1968), pp.
120–23.

31. *Disappearance,* p. 313.

32. "The Dialectic of Sense-Perception," *Hopkins, A Col-*

lection of Critical Essays, ed. Hartman (Englewood Cliffs, N. J.: Prentice-Hall, 1966), p. 121. We can understand why Hartman comes to the opposite conclusion—he deals with "The Windhover," which in this as in other respects is Hopkins's most successful poem. Here the pattern of stress, breaking, and release, which is manifest in the bird, the plowed field, and the embers, gives the poem a unity which "The Starlight Night" and most of the other sonnets lack. Even so we must rely on the epigraph and ultimately on the theological prose in order to understand that the tension signifies the Passion, the breaking the Crucifixion, and that the release is of the Holy Spirit.

33. Scotus II, 23 (*Opus Oxoniense,* I, d.1, p. 1, qu.2, n. 3).
34. *NV,* p. 13; *Disappearance,* p. 322.
35. Miller, *Disappearance,* pp. 314–15.

Chapter 5

1. *Degrees of Knowledge,* p. 324.
2. *Ibid.,* p. 253, 319.
3. *Ibid.,* p. 264.
4. *Ibid.,* pp. 261–62.
5. *Ibid.,* p. 253.
6. The exact extent of Newman's influence on Eliot is difficult to assess. Eliot alludes to him on several occasions, usually in reference to Newman's theory of assent, of which Eliot seems to have approved. See, for instance, the lecture on "Christianity and Communism," *Listener,* March, 1932, quoted by Kristian Smidt, *Poetry and Belief in the Work of T. S. Eliot* (London: Routledge and Kegan Paul, 1967), p. 28; and "The *Pensées* of Pascal," *Selected Essays,* p. 359. It also may be worth mentioning that there is a certain similarity between the two in their general attitudes and modes of approach to religious questions. These are sufficiently striking that Russell Kirk in *Eliot and His Age* (New York: Random House, 1971) finds it helpful to gloss a great many of Eliot's statements with pertinent passages from Newman. It may also be worth mentioning that

the Anglo-Catholicism of the 1920's and 30's, to which Eliot was converted, was to a much greater extent than that of the 1960's and 70's identified with an ecclesiastical party which was a direct extension of the Oxford Movement.

7. *The Criterion,* 5, (1927): 294–313. It is interesting that an essay by Maritain, "Poetry and Religion," appeared in *The Criterion* in the same year. References to *The Criterion* are to the "Collected Edition" (London: Faber and Faber, 1967).

8. *Ibid.,* 6: 340–42.

9. However, Ramon Fernandez, in a long article on Newman in *The Criterion* for October of 1924 (3: 84–102) discusses the question of whether or not Newman was a mystic (Fernandez concludes that he was not), and in October, 1927, back to back with his own response to Middleton Murry, Eliot prints his translation of Fernandez's response, "A Note on Intelligence and Intuition" (6: 332–39). In the latter essay Fernandez insists as does Eliot in his contribution to the debate that there is no generic difference between intuition and intelligence. The earlier essay on Newman insists on a distinction between mysticism and intelligence. It is difficult to believe that Eliot, as editor and translator, was allowing these distinctions to go unnoticed.

10. St. John of the Cross, *The Complete Works,* trans. E. Allison Peers (London: Burns, Oates & Washbourne, 1947), I, 22.

11. *Letters and Correspondence of John Henry Newman,* ed. Anne Mozley (London: Longmans, Green, 1911), II, 36.

12. *Understood* may not be the proper word. The attitudes reflected in the structure and texture of an image may not be fully conscious. On the other hand Eliot's imagery seems to bespeak full awareness of its implications.

13. Denis Donoghue, "T. S. Eliot's *Quartets:* A New Reading," *Four Quartets: a Casebook,* ed. Bernard Bergonzi (Nashville and London: Aurora, 1970), pp. 232–34.

14. St. John of the Cross, *Works,* I, 450–51. Italics added.

15. *T. S. Eliot, the Man and His Work,* ed. Allen Tate (New York: Delacorte, 1966), p. 81.

16. *The Invisible Poet: T. S. Eliot* (New York: Ivan Obolensky, 1959), p. 313.

17. *Essays,* pp. 562–65.

18. We should not omit all reference to Lady Juliana of Norwich whose *Revelations of Divine Love* echo in the *Quartets.* Indeed Eliot's return to the experience in respect of its meaning may owe something to her technique of narrating a vision and then proceeding to analyze its meaning.

Chapter 6

1. Maritain's primary works on art and poetry are *Art and Scholasticism,* edited in the same volume with the essay *The Frontiers of Poetry,* trans. Joseph W. Evans (New York: Scribner's, 1962) and *Creative Intuition in Art and Poetry* (New York: Pantheon, 1953). Gilson's books on artistic theory are *Painting and Reality* (New York: Pantheon, 1957); *The Arts of the Beautiful* (New York: Scribner's, 1965); and *Forms and Substances in the Arts,* trans. Salvator Attanasio (New York: Scribner's, 1966). These works will be cited in the text.

2. The book is co-authored by Maritain and his wife Raïssa, but the essay in question is by Maritain (New York: Philosophical Library, 1955).

3. *Ibid.,* pp. 50–51. Italics added.

4. *Ibid.,* p. 51. Cf. *Creative Intuition,* pp. 114–15.

5. There is a striking similarity between Maritain's "affective connaturality" and Newman's doctrine that the "whole man" reasons.

6. *Aristotle's Theory of Poetry and Fine Art* (New York: Dover, 1951), p. 154.

7. *The Poetry of Experience* (London: Chatto & Windus, 1957), p. 65. Italics added.

8. *Ibid.*

9. *Ibid.,* p. 46.

10. *Ibid.,* pp. 47, 69.

11. Gilson quotes from Aristotle's *Physics,* I, 9, 192a, 20–25.

12. In reference to these questions it is interesting to note that Gilson's allusions and citations indicate that he has been considerably influenced by the very school of poets whom we usually identify with the doctrine that words can be used without primary concern for meaning. I refer, of course, to the symbolists. That influence is certainly one explanation for his failure to deal adequately with the conceptual dimension of poetry. (We witness the same phenomenon in Maritain's work.)

13. The fullest discussion of this matter is Walter Clyde Curry's "Tumbling Nature's Germens" in *Shakespeare's Philosophical Patterns* (Baton Rouge: Louisiana State University Press, 1959), pp. 29–49.

14. C. S. Lewis, "Dante's Similes," *Studies in Medieval and Renaissance Literature,* ed. Walter Hooper (Cambridge: Cambridge University Press, 1966), pp. 75–76.

15. It is interesting that when Gilson deals with Dante's subject matter as a given rather than with a view to its justification as poetry, he does an excellent job of practical criticism. See his *Dante the Philosopher,* trans. David Moore (London: Sheed & Ward, 1948). In order to accommodate Dante's conceptual subject matter to the theory of creative intuition, in order to explain why we are "never bored with the philosophical lectures of Dante," Maritain is forced to speak of Dante's "innocence" and of his "luck." See *Creative Intuition,* pp. 370–87. The passage quoted is from p. 377.

Bibliography

Aquinas, St. Thomas. *Summa Contra Gentiles.* Translated by
Anton C. Pegis et al. 5 vols. Garden City, New York:
Doubleday, Image Books, 1955–1957.
————. *Summa Theologica.* Translated by the Fathers of the
English Dominican Province. 22 vols. London: Burns,
Oates & Washbourne, 1920–1925.
Bettoni, Efrem. *Duns Scotus: The Basic Principles of His
Philosophy.* Translated and edited by Bernardine Bonansea.
Washington: Catholic University of America Press, 1961.
Butcher, S. H. *Aristotle's Theory of Poetry and Fine Art with
a Critical Text and Translation of "The Poetics."* 4th ed.
New York: Dover, 1951.
Coogan, Marjorie D. "Inscape and Instress: Further Analogies
with Scotus." *PMLA* 65 (1950): 66–74.
Curry, Walter Clyde. *Shakespeare's Philosophical Patterns.*
2d ed. Baton Rouge: Louisiana State University Press, 1959.
Dante Alighieri. *La Divina Commedia.* Edited by C. H. Grand-
gent and revised by Charles S. Singleton. Cambridge: Har-
vard University Press, 1972.
————. *The Divine Comedy.* Translated by John D. Sinclair.
3 vols. New York: Oxford University Press, 1948.
Dawson, Christopher. "Newman and the Modern World."
The Tablet, 5 August, 1972, pp. 733–34.
Day, Sebastian J. *Intuitive Cognition, a Key to the Significance
of the Later Scholastics.* St. Bonaventure, N.Y.: The Fran-
ciscan Institute, 1947.
Devlin, Christopher, "An Essay on Scotus." *The Month* 182
(1946): 456–66.
————. "Hopkins and Duns Scotus." *New Verse* 14 (1935):
12–17.

―――. "The Image and the Word, I & II." *The Month* n.s. 3 (1950): 114–27; 191–202.

―――. "Time's Eunuch." *The Month* n.s. I (1949): 303–12.

Dobrée, Bonamy. "T. S. Eliot: A Personal Reminiscence." *T. S. Eliot: The Man and His Work.* Edited by Allen Tate. New York: Delacorte, 1966.

Donoghue, Denis. "T. S. Eliot's *Quartets:* A New Reading." *Four Quartets: A Casebook.* Edited by Bernard Bergonzi. Nashville and London: Aurora, 1970.

Eliot, T. S. *The Complete Poems and Plays, 1909–1950.* New York: Harcourt, Brace, 1952.

―――. "Mr. Middleton Murry's Synthesis." *The Criterion* 6 (1927): 340–47.

―――. *Selected Essays.* New York: Harcourt, Brace, 1950.

Fernandez, Ramon. "The Experience of Newman." *The Criterion* 3 (1924): 84–102.

―――. "A Note on Intelligence and Intuition." *The Criterion* 6 (1927): 332–39.

Gardner, W. H. *Gerard Manley Hopkins: A Study of Poetic Idiosyncrasy in Relation to Poetic Tradition.* 2d ed. 2 vols. London: Oxford University Press, 1966.

―――. "A Note on Hopkins and Duns Scotus." *Scrutiny* 5 (1936): 61–70.

Gilson, Etienne. *The Arts of the Beautiful.* New York: Charles Scribner's Sons, 1965.

―――. *The Christian Philosophy of St. Thomas Aquinas.* Translated by L. K. Shook. London: Victor Gollancz, 1961.

―――. *Dante the Philosopher.* Translated by David Moore. London: Sheed & Ward, 1948.

―――. *Forms and Substances in the Arts.* Translated by Salvator Attanasio. New York: Charles Scribner's Sons, 1966.

―――. *History of Christian Philosophy in the Middle Ages.* London: Sheed and Ward, 1955.

―――. *Jean Duns Scot, Introduction à ses positions fondamentales.* Paris: Librairie Philosophique J. Vrin, 1952.

―――. *Painting and Reality: The A. W. Mellon Lectures*

in the Fine Arts, 1955. Bollingen Series xxxv, 4. New York: Pantheon, 1957.

———. *Reason and Revelation in the Middle Ages.* New York: Charles Scribner's Sons, 1952.

———. *The Unity of Philosophical Experience.* London: Sheed & Ward, 1955.

Hartman, Geoffrey H., ed. *Hopkins: A Collection of Critical Essays.* Englewood Cliffs, N.J.: Prentice-Hall, A Spectrum Book, 1966.

Hopkins, Gerard Manley. *Further Letters of Gerard Manley Hopkins, Including His Correspondence with Coventry Patmore.* Edited by Claude Colleer Abbott. 2d ed., rev. London: Oxford University Press, 1956.

———. *The Journals and Papers of Gerard Manley Hopkins.* Edited by Humphry House and Graham Storey. London: Oxford University Press, 1959.

———. *The Poems of Gerard Manley Hopkins.* Edited by W. H. Gardner and N. H. Mackenzie. 4th ed., rev. London: Oxford University Press, 1967.

———. *The Sermons and Devotional Writings of Gerard Manley Hopkins.* Edited by Christopher Devlin. London: Oxford University Press, 1959.

St. John of the Cross. *The Complete Works.* Translated and edited by E. Allison Peers. 3 vols. London: Burns, Oates & Washbourne, 1947.

Kenner, Hugh. *The Invisible Poet: T. S. Eliot.* New York: Ivan Obolensky, 1959.

Kirk, Russell. *Eliot and His Age: T. S. Eliot's Moral Imagination in the Twentieth Century.* New York: Random House, 1971.

Langbaum, Robert. *The Poetry of Experience: The Dramatic Monologue in Modern Literary Tradition.* London: Chatto & Windus, 1957.

Lewis, C. S. "Dante's Similes." *Studies in Medieval and Renaissance Literature.* Edited by Walter Hooper. Cambridge: Cambridge University Press, 1966.

Maritain, Jacques. *Art and Scholasticism* and *The Frontiers of Poetry.* Translated by Joseph W. Evans. New York: Charles Scribner's Sons, The Scribner Library, 1962.

———. *Creative Intuition in Art and Poetry:* The A. W. Mellon Lectures in the Fine Arts. Bollingen Series xxxv, 1. New York: Pantheon, 1953.

———. *Distinguish to Unite or The Degrees of Knowledge.* Translated by Gerald B. Phelan. London: Geoffrey Bles, 1959.

Maritain, Jacques & Raïssa. *The Situation of Poetry: Four Essays on the Relations Between Poetry, Mysticism, Magic, and Knowledge.* Translated by Marshall Suther. New York: Philosophical Library, 1955.

Miller, J. Hillis. *The Disappearance of God: Five Nineteenth-Century Writers.* New York: Schocken, 1965.

Murry, John Middleton. "Towards a Synthesis." *The Criterion* 5 (1927): 294–313.

Newman, John Henry. *Apologia Pro Vita Sua, Being a History of His Religious Opinions.* Edited by Martin J. Svaglic. Oxford: Clarendon Press, 1967.

———. *An Essay in Aid of a Grammar of Assent.* Edited by Charles Frederick Harrold. London: Longmans, Green, 1947.

———. *Fifteen Sermons Preached Before the University of Oxford.* London: Longmans, Green, 1909.

———. *The Idea of a University Defined and Illustrated.* London: Longmans, Green, 1910.

———. *Lectures on the Doctrine of Justification.* London: Longmans, Green, 1908.

———. *Letters and Correspondence of John Henry Newman During His Life in the English Church.* Edited by Anne Mozley. 2 vols. London: Longmans, Green, 1911.

———. *The Philosophical Notebook of John Henry Newman.* Edited by Edward Sillem and revised by A. J. Boekraad. 2 vols. Louvain: Nauwelaerts, 1969–1970.

Pick, John. *Gerard Manley Hopkins, Priest and Poet.* 2d ed.

New York: Oxford University Press, A Galaxy Book, 1966.

Przywara, Erich. "St. Augustine and the Modern World." Translated by E. I. Watkin, in *Saint Augustine.* Cleveland and New York: World, Meridian Books, 1964.

Schneider, Elisabeth W. *The Dragon in the Gate: Studies in the Poetry of G. M. Hopkins.* Berkeley and Los Angeles: University of California Press, 1968.

Scoti, Ioannis Duns. *Opera Omnia.* Edited by P. Carolo Balić. Civitas Vaticana: Typis Polyglottis Vaticanis, 1950– .

Smidt, Kristian. *Poetry and Belief in the Work of T. S. Eliot.* 2d. ed., rev. London: Routledge and Kegan Paul, 1967.

Tate, Allen. *Essays of Four Decades.* Chicago: Swallow, 1968.

Index